# Lecture Notes in Computer Science   11235

Commenced Publication in 1973
Founding and Former Series Editors:
Gerhard Goos, Juris Hartmanis, and Jan van Leeuwen

Hakim Hacid · Quan Z. Sheng ·
Tetsuya Yoshida · Azadeh Sarkheyli ·
Rui Zhou (Eds.)

# Data Quality and Trust in Big Data

5th International Workshop, QUAT 2018
Held in Conjunction with WISE 2018
Dubai, UAE, November 12–15, 2018
Revised Selected Papers

 Springer

*Editors*
Hakim Hacid (ID)
Zayed University
Dubai, United Arab Emirates

Tetsuya Yoshida
Nara Women's University
Nara, Japan

Rui Zhou (ID)
Department of Computer Science
and Software Engineering
Swinburne University of Technology
Hawthorn, VIC, Australia

Quan Z. Sheng (ID)
Macquarie University
Sydney, NSW, Australia

Azadeh Sarkheyli (ID)
Dalarna University
Borlänge, Sweden

ISSN 0302-9743          ISSN 1611-3349  (electronic)
Lecture Notes in Computer Science
ISBN 978-3-030-19142-9          ISBN 978-3-030-19143-6  (eBook)
https://doi.org/10.1007/978-3-030-19143-6

LNCS Sublibrary: SL3 – Information Systems and Applications, incl. Internet/Web, and HCI

This Springer imprint is published by the registered company Springer Nature Switzerland AG
The registered company address is: Gewerbestrasse 11, 6330 Cham, Switzerland

# Preface

The series of WISE conferences aims to provide an international forum for researchers, professionals, and industrial practitioners to share their knowledge in the rapidly growing area of Web technologies, methodologies, and applications. The first WISE event took place in Hong Kong, China (2000). Then the trip continued to Kyoto, Japan (2001); Singapore (2002); Rome, Italy (2003); Brisbane, Australia (2004); New York, USA (2005); Wuhan, China (2006); Nancy, France (2007); Auckland, New Zealand (2008); Poznan, Poland (2009); Hong Kong, SAR China (2010); Sydney, Australia (2011); Paphos, Cyprus (2012); Nanjing, China (2013); Thessaloniki, Greece (2014); Miami, USA (2015); Shanghai, China (2016); Puschino, Russia (2017); and WISE 2018 was held in Dubai, UAE, supported by Zayed University.

The 5th WISE workshop on Data Quality and Trust in Big Data, QUAT 2018, was held in conjunction with WISE 2018, Dubai, UAE, during November 12–15, 2018. QUAT is a forum for presenting and discussing novel ideas and solutions related to the problems of exploring, assessing, monitoring, improving, and maintaining the quality of data and trust for "big data." It aims to provide the researchers in the areas of Web technology, e-services, social networking, big data, data processing, trust, and information systems and GIS a forum to discuss and exchange their recent research findings and achievements. This year, the QUAT 2018 program featured nine accepted papers on data cleansing, data quality analytics, reliability assessment, and quality of service for domain applications. QUAT 2018 was organized by Prof. Yuhao Wang, Prof. Martin Johanson, and Prof. William Song.

The problem of data quality in data processing, data management, data analysis, and information systems largely and indistinctly affects every application domain, especially in the era of big data. Big data has the characteristics of huge volumes of data and a great variety of structures or no structure. Big data is increased at a great velocity everyday and may be less trustable. The use of big data underpins critical activities in all sectors of our society. Many data-processing tasks (such as data collection, data integration, data sharing, information extraction, and knowledge acquisition) require various forms of data preparation and consolidation with complex data processing and analysis techniques. Achieving the full transformative potential of "big data" requires both new data analysis algorithms and a new class of systems to handle the dramatic data growth, the demand to integrate structured and unstructured data analytics, and the increasing computing needs of massive scale analytics. The consensus is that the quality of data and the veracity of data have to span over the entire process of data collection, preparation, analysis, modeling, implementation, use, testing, and maintenance, including novel algorithms and usable systems.

For the QUAT 2018 Workshop, we wish to thank the general co-chairs, Prof. Yuhao Wang, Prof. Martin Johanson, and Prof. William Song; the Program Committee chairs, Prof. Wei Huang, Prof. Siril Yella, and Dr. Roger G. Nyberg; and the Organizing Committee members, Dr. Xiaoyun Zhao, Prof. Hong Rao, and Dr. Azadeh Sarkheyli.

We also wish to take this opportunity to thank the WISE Organizing Committee: the general co-chairs, Prof. Zakaria Maamar and Prof. Marek Rusinkiewicz; the program co-chairs, Prof. Hakim Hacid, Prof. Wojciech Cellary, and Prof. Hua Wang; the workshop co-chairs, Prof. Michael Sheng and Prof. Tetsuya Yoshida; the tutorial and panel chair, Dr. Hye-Young Helen Paik; the sponsor chair, Dr. Fatma Taher; the finance chair, Prof. Hakim Hacid; the local arrangements co-chairs, Dr. Andrew Leonce, Prof. Huwida Saeed, and Prof. Emad Bataineh; the publication chair, Dr. Rui Zhou; the publicity co-chairs, Dr. Dickson Chiu, Dr. Reda Bouadjenek, and Dr. Vanilson Burégio; the website co-chairs, Mr. Emir Ugljanin and Mr. Emerson Bautista; and the WISE Steering Committee representative, Prof. Yanchun Zhang.

In addition, special thanks are due to the members of the international Program Committee and the external reviewers for a rigorous and robust reviewing process. We are also grateful to Zayed University, UAE; Complex Systems & Microdata Analysis, Dalarna University, Sweden; School of Information Engineering, Nanchuang University, China; Springer Nature Switzerland AG; and the international WISE society for supporting this workshop. The WISE Organizing Committee is also grateful to the workshop organizers for their great efforts to help promote Web information system research to broader domains.

We expect that the ideas that have emerged at in QUAT 2018 will result in the development of further innovations for the benefit of scientific, industrial, and social communities.

March 2019

Hakim Hacid
Quan Z. Sheng
Tetsuya Yoshida
Azadeh Sarkheyli
Rui Zhou

# QUAT Organization

## QUAT General Co-chairs

Yuhao Wang      Nanchang University, China
Martin Johanson      Dalarna University, Sweden
William Song      Dalarna University, Sweden

## QUAT Program Committee Co-chairs

Wei Huang      Nanchang University, China
Siril Yella      Dalarna University, Sweden
Roger G. Nyberg      Dalarna University, Sweden

## QUAT Organizing Committee Co-chairs

Xiaoyun Zhao      Dalarna University, Sweden
Hong Rao      Nanchang University, China
Azadeh Sarkheyli      Dalarna University, Sweden

## QUAT Program Committee

| | |
|---|---|
| Anders G. Nilsson | Stockholm University, Sweden |
| David Budgen | Durham University, UK |
| Christer Carlsson | Åbo Akademi University, Finland |
| Deren Chen | Zhejiang University, China |
| Hercules Dalianis | Stockholm University, Sweden |
| Xiaofeng Du | British Telecom, UK |
| Hasan Fleyeh | Dalarna University, Sweden |
| Johan Håkansson | Dalarna University, Sweden |
| Paul Johannesson | Stockholm University, Sweden |
| Michael Lang | National University of Ireland Galway, Ireland |
| Yang Li | British Telecom, UK |
| Henry Linger | Monash University, Australia |
| Christer Magnusson | Stockholm University, Sweden |
| Malcolm Munro | Durham University, UK |
| Jaroslav Pokorny | Charles University in Prague, Czech Republic |
| William Song | Dalarna, Sweden |
| Bo Sundgren | Stockholm University, Sweden |
| Hua Wang | Victoria University, Australia |
| Xiaolin Zheng | Zhejing University, China |
| Sheng Zhang | Nanchang Hangkong University, China |
| Benting Wan | Jiangxi University of Finance and Economics, China |

| Sheng Zhang | Jiangxi Hangkong University, China |
| Shaozhong Zhang | Zhejiang Wanli University, China |
| Qingshan Deng | Jiangxi University of Finance and Economics, China |
| Zichen Xu | Nanchang University, China |

## QUAT Sponsors

Complex Systems & Microdata Analysis, Dalarna University, Sweden
School of Information Engineering, Nanchuang University, China

# Contents

# A Novel Data Quality Metric
# for Minimality

Lisa Ehrlinger[1,2(✉)] and Wolfram Wöß[1]

[1] Johannes Kepler University Linz, Linz, Austria
{lisa.ehrlinger,wolfram.woess}@jku.at
[2] Software Competence Center Hagenberg, Hagenberg im Mühlkreis, Austria
lisa.ehrlinger@scch.at

**Abstract.** The development of well-founded metrics to measure data quality is essential to estimate the significance of data-driven decisions, which are, besides others, the basis for artificial intelligence applications. While the majority of research into data quality refers to the data values of an information system, less research is concerned with schema quality. However, a poorly designed schema negatively impacts the quality of the data, for example, redundancies at the schema-level lead to inconsistencies and anomalies at the data-level. In this paper, we propose a new metric to measure the minimality of a schema, which is an important indicator to detect redundancies. We compare it to other minimality metrics and show that it is the only one that fulfills all requirements for a sound data quality metric. In our ongoing research, we are evaluating the benefits of the metric in more detail and investigate its applicability for redundancy detection in data values.

## 1 Introduction

Poor data quality (DQ) leads to effects like cost increase, customer dissatisfaction, and organizational mistrust [1], which is why DQ has become critical for operational excellence [2]. Data quality is usually perceived as multidimensional concept that is characterized by different aspects, so called *dimensions* [3]. Those dimensions can either refer to the *extension* of the data (i.e., data values), or to their *intension* (i.e., the schema) [4]. While the majority of research into DQ focuses on the data values [4,5], the minimality metric in this paper has been originally developed for schema quality. The DQ dimension *minimality* (also uniqueness, non-redundancy, compactness, or conciseness) describes the capability of a schema to represent the aspects of the reality of interest with the minimal use of information sources [4]. In other words, a schema is considered minimal if there are no redundancies, i.e., no elements that can be omitted without loosing information [4]. This quality dimension is of particular interest in the context of integrated information systems (IIS), where redundant representations are common due to autonomous information sources.

A schema of an information system (IS) describes the data structure and its relationships [6] and can also be denoted as *metadata*. The concepts a schema

© Springer Nature Switzerland AG 2019
H. Hacid et al. (Eds.): QUAT 2018, LNCS 11235, pp. 1–15, 2019.
https://doi.org/10.1007/978-3-030-19143-6_1

consists of are also called "schema elements", and are, for example tables in a relational database (DB), or classes in an ontology. The quality of conceptual and logical schemas is essential for IS development, since an erroneous schema design strongly impacts the quality of an IS and its data values [4]. Additionally, it is important to regularly reassess schema quality, since changes during runtime can negatively affect the quality even if the initial schema had an ideal design. Thus, we aim at an automated approach to schema minimality measurement by focusing on machine-readable logical schemas from productive ISs in contrast to conceptual schema models. A typical use case for the application of our metric is a productive Big Data IIS, which contains current as well as legacy data from different sources. In such a scenario, manual DQ assessment by a domain expert is often not possible.

The contribution of this paper is a novel metric to measure the DQ dimension *minimality* on schema-level. The key benefit of our metric is an automated, repeated calculation that supports continuous DQ measurement, which ensures that DQ continues to conform to requirements over time. We compare our metric to existing ones and show that it is the only metric that fulfills all five requirements by Heinrich et al. [7] and copes with corner cases appropriately. For demonstration and evaluation purposes, we implemented the metric as part of the previously developed DQ tool QuaIIe [8]. In our ongoing research, we are evaluating the benefits of the metric in more detail and investigate its applicability for redundancy detection in data values.

The remainder of this paper is structured as follows: first, we present our new minimality metric in Sect. 2 and evaluate it in Sect. 3. A discussion of related research work with respect to the DQ dimension *minimality* as well as more scientific background into hierarchical clustering is provided in Sect. 4. We conclude in Sect. 5.

## 2    A Novel Minimality Metric

Our proposed minimality calculation can be summarized in three steps. Details on hierarchical clustering and similarity calculation are provided in Sect. 4.

1. *Similarity calculation.* The similarity between all elements within a schema needs to be computed with a suitable similarity or distance function. In this paper, a similarity function $\sigma : e \times e \rightarrow \mathbb{R} \in [0, 1]$ defines the closeness between two elements, where 1.0 denotes a perfect match and 0.0 complete dissimilarity [9].
2. *Clustering.* All schema elements are hierarchically clustered according to their similarity values. In a perfectly minimal schema, the number of clusters $|c|$ should be equal into the number of elements $|e|$. If two or more elements are grouped together into one cluster, the minimality score drops below 1.0.

3. *Minimality calculation.* Finally, the minimality of a schema $s$ is calculated according to

$$Min(s) = \frac{|\text{unique}(e)|}{|e|} = \begin{cases} 1.0, & \text{if } |e| = 1 \\ \frac{|c|-1}{|e|-1}, & \text{else} \end{cases}. \tag{1}$$

In contrast to Batista and Salgado [10], who count redundant elements $red(e)$, we suggest counting the unique elements $unique(e)$ by grouping similar elements into clusters. Our design decision has the following three advantages when compared to existing metrics:

**Ratio-Scaled Metric.** In contrast to existing metrics, our metric fulfills all requirements for well-founded DQ metrics, which have been proposed by Heinrich et al. [7]. The minimality metric even achieves the ratio scale, which is a measurement scale with a defined zero point [11]. These statements are further justified in Sect. 3 by means of Fig. 1.

**Resolution of Multi-correspondences.** A multi-correspondence describes the case where three or more elements have a very high similarity to each other and it is not clear which two of them to mark as "redundant". The resolution of multi-correspondences is considered a challenge in similarity calculation [9] and is often not considered in related work (cf. [10]). Hierarchical clustering resolves multiple correspondences by assigning very similar elements (independently of the number) to the same group or cluster [12].

**Concept of Uniqueness.** In contrast to "uniqueness" (i.e., counting unique elements by clustering), the concept of "redundancy" (i.e., marking two very similar elements as redundant) is not clearly defined in [10]. Batista and Salgado [10] stated that an entity is considered fully redundant when all of its attributes are redundant. Further, they claimed that only one attribute out of two semantically equivalent ones is marked as redundant, while the other one is kept in the schema to assure that no domain information is lost. An explanation of the process for selecting which attribute (out of a pair of two equivalent attributes) should be removed, is also missing. According to these assumptions, a schema element cannot reach full redundancy if the redundant attributes are assigned to the same element. For example, in the case where the schema element actor has two redundant attributes country1 and country2, only one attribute (e.g., country1) would count as redundant element $red(e)$. This would lead to a minimality rating of 0.5 in the worst case, where all attributes of an element are fully redundant.

# 3    Evaluation and Discussion of the Minimality Metric

In this section, we evaluate our minimality metric by comparing it to existing ones (cf. Subsect. 3.1) and by discussing its properties and justifying the design decisions, for example, the reason behind the "$-1$" in Eq. 1. In addition, we show how to apply our metric with the general-purpose DQ tool QuaIIe [8], where we evaluated the measurement results by comparing it to expert ratings.

## 3.1    Existing Schema Minimality Metrics

Batista and Salgado [10,13,14] proposed an approach to measure and enhance the quality of schemas in an integrated IS by means of three metrics for the quality dimensions completeness, minimality, and type consistency. The mentioned minimality metric is the closest to our proposal that we found in literature. Since [10,13,14] contain overlapping information with respect to the description of the metric and the concept of redundancy, we refer in the following to [10]. Batista and Salgado [10] suggested calculating minimality according to

$$Mi_{S_m} = 1 - \frac{|red(e)|}{|e|} = 1 - [ER(S_m) + RR(S_m)], \tag{2}$$

where $|red(e)|$ is the number of redundant schema elements and $|e|$ the total number of elements in an integrated schema $S_m$. The metric is applied by computing entity redundancy $ER$ and relationship redundancy $RR$ according to

$$ER(S_m) = \frac{\sum_{k=1}^{n_m} Red(E_k, S_m)}{n_m}, \tag{3}$$

$$RR(S_m) = \frac{\sum_{l=1}^{n_{rel}} \#Red(R_l, S_m)}{n_{rel}}, \tag{4}$$

where $n_m$ is the number of entities and $n_{rel}$ the total number of relationships in $S_m$. The hash ($\#$) in $RR(S_m)$ of Eq. 4 indicates the number of redundant relationships and therefore duplicates the sum sign. Note that Eq. 2 does not normalize to a value in the range $[0,1]$, as the sum of $ER$ and $RR$ can reach a maximum value of 2 (leading to $Mi_{S_m} = 1 - 2 = -1$). An example for the minimality calculation in Section 6.1 of Batista and Salgado's work [10] yields normalized results, which does however not correspond to the formulas. In 2008, the metrics for $ER$ and $RR$ were refined in Batista's PhD thesis [5] to Eqs. 5 and 6 in an attempt to normalize the final minimality and removing the hash:

$$ER(S_m) = \frac{\sum_{k=1}^{n_m} Red(E_k, S_m)}{n_m + n_{rel}}, \tag{5}$$

$$RR(S_m) = \frac{\sum_{j=1}^{n_{rel}} Red(R_j, S_m)}{n_{rel} + n_m}. \tag{6}$$

In the following example, we show that the normalization is still not achieved in the refined version. Assuming that a schema contains 5 entities and 7 relationships, where one entity is marked as redundant, the minimality would be calculated as follows:

$$ER(S_m) = \frac{1}{(5+7)} = 0.0833$$

$$RR(S_m) = \frac{0}{(7+5)} = 0$$

$$Mi_{S_m} = 1 - [0.0833 + 0] = 0.926$$

Equations 5 and 6 introduce an impact of the number of relationships $n_{rel}$ to entity redundancy and vice versa (the number of entities $n_m$ affects relationship redundancy). Reducing the number of relationships in the example to 4 would increase $ER$ to 0.1111 and consequently decrease schema minimality to 0.8889. To remove this undesired effect, we suggest calculating $ER$ and $RR$ in this context according to the original equations in [10], but refining schema minimality according to Eq. 7. This leads to constant redundancy values for $ER$ and $RR$ and removes the impact of the respective other number of elements.

$$Mi_{S_m} = 1 - \left[\frac{ER(S_m) + RR(S_m)}{2}\right] \tag{7}$$

Duchateau and Bellahense [15] presented an approach to measure the quality (including completeness, minimality, and structurality) of schema-matching results compared to an expert-created reference schema. Although the authors claimed to have adopted the minimality calculation from [10], their formula

$$min(Si_{tool}, Si_{exp}) = 1 - \frac{|Si_{tool}| - |Si_{tool} \cap Si_{exp}|}{|Si_{exp}|} \tag{8}$$

deviates notably because it requires a reference schema $Si_{exp}$ for calculating the minimality of the observed schema $Si_{tool}$. $|Si|$ is the number of elements in schema $Si$. In contrast, we aim at measuring the minimality of schemas without considering a perfect reference (i.e., a gold standard), because it usually does not exist in practical scenarios, such as, productive Big Data IS.

## 3.2   Discussion of the Metric Properties

Table 1 lists the metrics we consider for our evaluation. The first two metrics are derived from [10]. While M1 corresponds exactly to Eq. 2 by [10], we additionally added M2, which is a modification of M1 that aligns with the statement "that only one [attribute out of two] must be marked as redundant" [10]. Consequently, we tackle the ambiguity of the redundancy definition by considering both possibilities: when counting the redundant elements $|red(e)|$, either two out of two corresponding elements are counted (M1), or only one element is counted for two corresponding ones (M2). In addition, we added our cluster-based metric in three different versions to show the effect of the $-1$ shift (M3-5). In Table 1, the case "if $|e| = 1$" from Eq. 1 is omitted to demonstrate its need.

**Table 1.** Minimality metrics with respect to corner cases

| Number | M1 | M2 | M3 | M4 | M5 |
|--------|----|----|----|----|----|
| Metric | $1 - \frac{|red(e)|}{|e|}$ | $1 - \frac{2*|red(e)|}{|e|}$ | $\frac{|c|}{|e|}$ | $\frac{|c|+1}{|e|+1}$ | $\frac{|c|-1}{|e|-1}$ |
| C0 | NaN | NaN | NaN | 1.00 | 1.00 |
| C1 | 1.00 | 1.00 | 1.00 | 1.00 | NaN |

**Corner Cases.** To provide a sound metric, corner cases need to be considered. Table 1 lists the results of the metrics with respect to two corner cases: (C0) is an empty schema that contains no elements, and (C1) is a schema with only one element. C0 shows that all metrics (M1-3) that have $|e|$ in the denominator can not be calculated on an empty schema due to a division by zero. However, due to the $-1$ shift, M5 yields NaN for C1. Consequently, those corner cases must be handled explicitly, which justifies the special case $|e| = 1$ in Eq. 1.

**DQ Metric Requirements.** Heinrich et al. [7] defined five requirements ($R1$-$5$) a DQ metric should fulfill to adequately support decision-making. The authors point out that the requirements have been developed for metrics concerning the quality on the data-level and might not be directly applied to metrics for schema-level quality. Since there are no comparable requirements for schema quality metrics, we use [7] for our evaluation, along with comments on the relevance of the respective requirements. The basis for this investigation is shown in Fig. 1, where a boxplot summarizes the properties (minimum, maximum, and mean) of all possible results a metric yields. The evaluation has been performed on a schema with 30 elements and demonstrates all possible result combinations, independently of the used similarity function or clustering strategy. In the following paragraphs, we discuss the fulfillment of the requirements for M1-5.

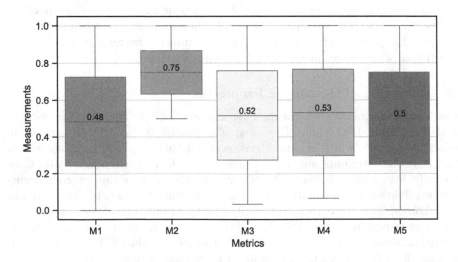

**Fig. 1.** Comparison of minimality metrics

*(R1) Existence of Minimum and Maximum Metric Values.* This requirement states that the metric values need to be bounded from below and from above in order to attain both a minimum (representing perfectly poor data quality) and a maximum (representing perfectly good data quality) [7]. Such a bounding is necessary to compare metric values over time and to observe an improvement of the measure. In our context, a bounding by $[0, 1]$ is desired, where 1 represents perfect minimality and 0 absolute redundancy in the schema. Figure 1 shows that only M1 and M5 are bound by $[0, 1]$ and, thus, fulfill R1.

M3 demonstrates the need for the shift by $-1$ in Eq. 1. In the case of "perfectly poor quality" all elements are completely redundant and therefore grouped into one cluster. Thus, the number of clusters $|c|$ cannot reach a value below 1.0, which is why M3 yields in the worst case $\frac{1}{|e|}$ and can never reach 0.0. M2, which aligns with the statement "that only one [attribute out of two] must be marked as redundant" [10], leads to a minimum metric value of 0.5.

*(R2) Interval-Scaled Metric Values.* To evaluate changes in the quality, it is necessary that the units along the metric scale are equally spaced [7]. This requirement describes the desire to determine the intervals of the metric values in a meaningful way, based on the classification of measurement scales [7]. The interval scale is more powerful than nominal and ordinal measurement scales, because it captures information about the size of the intervals that separate the single interval units. This characteristic allows to understand the "jump" (i.e., difference) from one unit to another [11].

M1 is the only metric that does not fulfill R2, because it yields a mean of 0.48 despite being bound by $[0, 1]$. This is caused by the concept of redundancy, which is a property that involves at least two elements, thus, the case in which $|red(e)|$ equals to $|e| - 1$ can never be reached. For example, in a schema with 5 elements, M1 yields the following possible results: $\{0.0, 0.2, 0.4, 0.6, 1.0\}$. Consequently, the distance between perfect minimality (1.0) and the next lower unit on the metric scale is always twice as long as between all other units. M2 shows that if redundancy is interpreted differently (i.e., only one element is marked redundant), R2 can be fulfilled.

In contrast to M3 and M4 (which are also interval-scaled), our proposed metric M5 achieves the ratio scale, which is an even stricter measurement scale with a defined zero point [11]. A ratio scale preserves ordering, the size of the intervals as well as ratios between the units. The key feature, which distinguishes the ratio scale from weaker measurement scales (nominal, ordinal, and interval) is the existence of empirical relations to capture ratios, e.g., "twice as redundant" [11].

*(R3) Quality of the Configuration Parameters and Determination of the Metric values.* This requirement states that is needs to be possible to determine the configuration and determination parameters of a DQ metric according to the quality criteria objectivity, reliability, and validity [7]. R3 is fulfilled by all five metrics since all parameters can be determined automatically, and are thus objective, reliable, and valid. The number of schema elements ($|e|$) can be simply

counted, while redundant elements $(red(e))$ and unique elements, i.e., clusters $(c)$ can be determined using an appropriate similarity or distance function.

*(R4) Sound Aggregation of the Metric Values.* This requirement states that a DQ metric must be applicable not only to single data values, but also to sets of data values (e.g., tuples, relations, and a whole database) and that the aggregated metric values need to be consistent throughout all levels [7]. Since our metric was originally developed for schema quality measurement, R4 cannot be directly used for our evaluation. For all five schema quality metrics observed in this paper (M1-5) there is no need for further aggregation, since the entire schema is targeted. However, information about the DB content could be integrated in the metrics by tuning the respective similarity/distance functions. We conclude that this requirement is not relevant for our work.

*(R5) Economic Efficiency of the Metric.* The expected return on investment (ROI) from applying the metric has to be economically efficient, that is, the benefit has to outweight the expected costs for determining the configuration parameters and the metric values [7]. We do not consider this requirement as relevant for our work, because we focus on the technical soundness of the metric. However, we argue that R5 is fulfilled for all five metrics, since in accordance with R4, the employed configuration parameters can be determined automatically by means of similarity/distance functions or counting.

We conclude that M5 is the only metric that fulfills all requirements by Heinrich et al. [7]. Since our research focuses on a technically sound measurement, we consider the normalization (R1) and the interval-scaling (R2) as most important in contrast to the other requirements.

### 3.3 Application of the Minimality Metric with QuaIIe

The minimality metric proposed in this paper has been implemented and evaluated in the Java-based tool QuaIIe (Quality Assessment for Integrated Information Environments, pronounced [ˈkvɑlə]), which supports quality measurements at the data- and schema-level [8]. To overcome data model heterogeneity of different IS schemas, the tool creates a harmonized machine-readable description for each schema using the (data source description) vocabulary [16]. Quality measurements are then annotated to the respective elements in the schema descriptions and can be exported using an XML report or stored in a DB to continuously monitor the DQ over time. For the evaluation in this paper, we used the following DBs:

- *Alphavantage* is highly volatile and real-world stock exchange data, which we collected using the Alphavantage API[1].
- *Chinook*[2] is a relational sample DB for digital media.

---

[1] https://www.alphavantage.co [December, 2018].
[2] https://archive.codeplex.com/?p=chinookdatabase [December, 2018].

- *Employees*[3] is a sample DB by MySQL with six tables and about three million records that stores employees and departments within a company. We selected the employees schema due to a special case, where the parallel associations `dept_emp` (assignment of an employee to a department) and `dept_manager` (assignment of a manager, which is also stored in the employees table, to a department) model two semantically different roles between the same entity types. Although there is no semantic redundancy, the two relations have a very high similarity and are suited to demonstrate our minimality metric.
- *Northwind*[4] is the well-known MS SQL DB from Microsoft.
- *Metadynea* is a productive Cassandra DB from one of our industry partners, which stores about 60 GB of chemometrics data distributed on three nodes.
- *Sakila*[5] is a DB for the administration of a film distribution, which has also been published by MySQL. Compared to the employees DB, it has less records, but a more advanced schema with 16 tables.

For the evaluation of our minimality metric, we aimed at using both: common synthetic data sets as well as large real world data sets. Synthetic data sets with a well-known qualitative condition allow manual tracking and verification of the performed calculations. In addition, we also wanted to demonstrate the applicability of the metric to real-world data, which has the drawback that it is not possible to publish the schema in all cases (e.g., the metadynea schema).

Hierarchical clustering as it is implemented in QuaIIe requires three parameters to be selected: (1) a similarity or distance function, (2) a cluster heterogeneity threshold, and (3) a cluster linkage strategy. All three parameters are described in more detail in Sect. 4. To calculate the similarity between the schema elements for this evaluation, we used "DSD similarity", which is described along with a standard parameter evaluation in [17]. Note, however, that the minimality metric can likewise be calculated with any other similarity function as demonstrated in [17]. Additionally, we used a cluster heterogeneity threshold of 0.85. The linkage strategy defines the technique used to merge the single elements into clusters and while QuaIIe offers a selection of different strategies, we used the single-link strategy for the evaluations in this work.

To assess the usability of the measurement results, five IS experts rated the fulfillment of the minimality rating for the respective IS schemas intuitively with a number between 1.0 (complete fulfillment) and 0.0 (not fulfilled at all) as well as a self-assessment regarding their expertise. We computed a "target measurement", which is the weighted average of all expert's assessment, where the expertise was used as weight. Table 2 compares the minimality ratings measured with QuaIIe ($Min_{QuaIIe}$) to the expert ratings ($Min_{Exp}$), where it can be seen that the minimality measures generally reflect the expert perception quite well.

---

[3] https://dev.mysql.com/doc/employee/en [December, 2018].

[4] https://docs.microsoft.com/en-us/dotnet/framework/data/adonet/sql/linq/ downloading-sample-databases [December, 2018].

[5] https://dev.mysql.com/doc/sakila/en [December, 2018].

**Table 2.** Minimality measurement evaluations

| IS Schema | $Min_{QualIe}$ | $Min_{Exp}$ |
|---|---|---|
| Alphavantage | 1.000 | 1.000 |
| Chinook | 1.000 | 1.000 |
| Employees | 0.800 | 0.973 |
| Northwind | 1.000 | 1.000 |
| Metadynea | 0.667 | 0.696 |
| Sakila | 1.000 | 1.000 |

All except two schemas achieve the perfect minimality, which was also confirmed by the expert ratings. In an exemplary drill-down of the Sakila schema, it can be seen that all schema elements are sufficiently different to each other and are therefore assigned to separate clusters, which is why minimality is calculated according to $\frac{16-1}{16-1} = 1.0$. The low rating for the metadynea schema is expected, because it is a Cassandra DB schema, where denormalization (and thus, redundancy at the schema-level) is an intended design decision. The second schema, which did no achieve perfect minimality is the employees DB, where the two relations `dept_emp` and `dept_manager` achieve a very high similarity of 0.875. This reduces the minimality rating to $\frac{5-1}{6-1} = 0.8$. In practice, such a rating indicates an IS architect that the two associations should be further analyzed. However, in our case, no further action is required since the employees schema contains a special modeling concept of parallel associations (i.e., two different roles) which does not represent semantic redundancy, but leads to very similar relations in the schema model. Interestingly, the special case in the employees DB was also recognized by two experts, but with far less impact.

The minimality calculations from this paper can be reconstructed with the program `QualIe.jar` and the employed DSD schema description files, which are published on our project website[6]. The quality reports for the demo can be generated by executing "`java -jar QualIe.jar <schema>.ttl`".

## 4    Related Work and Scientific Background

This section first discusses the DQ dimension *minimality* and how it is currently perceived in existing research. Second, we present the necessary scientific background on hierarchical clustering, which is required to apply the minimality metric proposed in this paper. To the end, we present an outlook on how our schema minimality metric could be applied to measure redundancy on the data-level of ISs, that is, to calculate an index for duplicate detection.

---

[6] http://dqm.faw.jku.at [December, 2018].

## 4.1    Data Quality and the Minimality Dimension

Data quality is traditionally described as multi-dimensional concept, where each DQ dimension describes a different aspect of an information system's quality [4,18–20]. Those aspects can either refer to the data values (extension), or to their schema (intension) [4]. Although the metric presented in this paper has been originally developed for schema quality, we observe the DQ dimension *minimality* in this subsection from a more general perspective to demonstrate the potential of the metric for an application on the data-level as well. We also want to point out that there is no agreed-on standard of DQ dimensions, which is why, the desire for data to be non-redundant or minimal is described differently in existing research.

DQ dimensions can be quantified with DQ *metrics*, which capture the fulfillment of the dimensions in numerical values [21]. Well-founded DQ metrics are required for two major reasons [7]: (1) they indicate the extent to which decision makers can rely on the underlying data values, and (2) they support an economically oriented management of data quality. While there has been much research on metrics for DQ dimensions like accuracy, completeness, correctness, consistency, and timeliness (cf. [7,22]), the aspect of *minimality* was so far only observed on schema-level in [10] and [15] and has not reached sufficient attention on the data-level. However, the amount of research into *duplicate detection* shows the relevance and importance of this aspect to the general topic of data quality. While Piro et al. [19] agree that duplicate detection is a practical problem, they state that it is a *symptom* of DQ and no dimension. Neither the ISO 25012 standard on DQ [23], nor Myers [20] in his "List of Conformed Dimensions of Data Quality" include a dimension, which describes the desire of data to be non-redundant or unique.

In this section, we want to highlight the paradox that there exists no agreed-on DQ dimension for non-redundancy or minimality of data, and consequently no metric for repetitive measurement has been proposed. Thus, in the following, we list selected definitions of the concept of *minimality* and synonymous and related terms how they appear in literature:

- *Concise representation* is mentioned as DQ dimension that is not described any further (Pipino et al. [24]).
- *Conciseness* has been identified as data-related DQ dimension, which was cited two times in related work (Wand and Wang [18]).
- *Entity uniqueness*: no entity exists more than once within a system (Loshin [25]).
- *Non-duplication* is mentioned as DQ dimension (English [26]).
- *Minimality*: a description of the degree up to which undesired redundancy is avoided during the data extraction and source integration process (Jarke et al. [27]).
- *Minimum redundancy* (Redman 1996).
- *Redundancy*, minimality, compactness, and conciseness refer to the capability of representing the aspects of the reality of interest with the minimal use of informative resources (Batini and Scannapieco [4]).

- *Uniqueness* is the state of being the only one of its kind. Being without an equal or equivalent (Cykana et al. [28]).
- *Uniqueness*: no thing will be recorded more than once based upon how that thing is identified (DAMA UK [29]).

We conclude that while minimality is an accepted dimension at the schema-level to detect redundancies [4], so far there is no agreed-on DQ dimension (nor metric) that describes the desire for data to be minimal, that is, non-redundant, or unique. This is noteworthy, because duplicate detection is an important topic in DQ research. However, the dimension we presented in this paper is general enough to be applied not only on the schema-level, but on the data-level as well, which is part of our ongoing research work.

## 4.2 Hierarchical Clustering

Clustering describes the unsupervised process of classifying patterns into groups, i.e., the *clusters* [12]. Jain et al. [12] provide a comprehensive overview on clustering algorithms in general and details into hierarchical clustering in particular. In the following paragraphs, we describe the most important variables that need to be selected to perform hierarchical clustering: (1) the elements and features to be clustered, (2) a similarly or distance function, (3) a cluster heterogeneity threshold, and (4) the cluster linkage strategy.

In our schema-level minimality calculation, the schema descriptions are available as DSD description files, and thus, all schema elements are described by a standardized set of parameters. Further information on the used feature vectors is provided in [17]. For other application scenarios, like duplicate detection, it is previously required to define the properties of the records used for clustering in order to apply a distance function.

Most hierarchical clustering algorithms use distance or similarity functions for clustering, although this is not necessarily required. Other possibilities to construct the hierarchy are density- or graph-based methods [30]. For our work, we define a similarity function as the closeness between two elements $\sigma : e \times e \rightarrow \mathbb{R} \in [0,1]$, where 1.0 is a perfect match and 0.0 complete dissimilarity. A similarity value can be transformed into a distance value using $\delta = 1 - \sigma$ [9]. A hierarchical clustering algorithm can be visualized with a *dendrogram*, which represents the similarity levels at which groupings change [12]. Figure 2 shows the dendrogram of the employees DB clustering.

The threshold defines the minimum similarity value between two elements such that they are grouped together into the same cluster [30]. As indicated in Fig. 2, the standard threshold is set to 0.85. Thus, the two elements dept_emp and dept_manager with a similarity of 0.875 are grouped together into one cluster, while all other elements are assigned to separate clusters.

On a more general level, is distinguished between two types of hierarchical clustering, depending on how the cluster tree is constructed: (1) *agglomerative* or bottom-up methods, where single elements are merged into higher-level clusters,

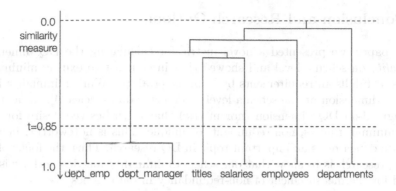

**Fig. 2.** Dendrogram of clustering employees DB

and (2) *divisive* or top-down methods [30], where the sum of elements is successively divided into smaller sub-parts. Since we start with the single (schema) elements, we use an agglomerative method. Here, the main challenge is to select a proper objective function to decide how to merge the single elements. The linkage strategy defines the technique used to merge the single elements into clusters. In order to select an appropriate cluster linkage strategy, we evaluated the following six strategies, which are implemented in QuaIIe: (1) single linkage, (2) complete linkage, (3) centroid linkage, (4) median linkage, and (5) Ward's method. Despite small variances in the cluster building, there was no difference in the final minimality rating.

## 4.3 Minimality Metric on Data-Level: An Outlook

In contrast to the application on schema-level as described in Sect. 3.3, an application of our minimality metric on the data-level would require the selection of different features on the input-side. First, instead of schema elements, records need to be clustered. Depending on the kind of records, an appropriate distance function needs to be developed. It is necessary to define a distance function that takes into account the different data types of the attributes. For example, to calculate the distance between persons in a person table, a string distance could be applied to the first and last name and a distance for numeric attributes to the age, while giving higher weights to the name than the age. QuaIIe implements a number of distance functions, for example, the affine gap distance, cosine distance, and Levenshtein distance for strings, and an absolute value distance for double values. In practice, the ensemble distance is used, which is a weighted-average of individual attribute distance functions [8].

We are currently performing tests on the automated selection of the appropriate distance function for each data type, to provide an initial suggestion of an ensemble distance, which can then be adjusted to the users needs.

# 5   Conclusion and Research Outlook

In this paper, we presented a novel metric for calculating the DQ dimension *minimality* on schema-level and showed that in contrast to exiting minimality metrics, it fulfills all requirements by Heinrich et al. [7]. While minimality is an accepted dimension at the schema-level to detect redundancies [4], so far there is no agreed-on DQ dimension (nor metric) that describes the desire for data to be minimal, that is, non-redundant, or unique. This is noteworthy, because duplicate detection is an important topic in DQ research. Thus, the focus of our ongoing research is to show that our schema minimality metric can likewise be applied for the measurement of non-redundancy in data values.

**Acknowledgments.** The research reported in this paper has been supported by the Austrian Ministry for Transport, Innovation and Technology, the Federal Ministry of Digital and Economic Affairs, and the Province of Upper Austria in the frame of the COMET center SCCH. In addition, the authors would like to thank Bernhard Werth and Thomas Grubinger for their valuable feedback on this work.

# References

1. Redman, T.C.: The impact of poor data quality on the typical enterprise. Commun. ACM **41**(2), 79–82 (1998)
2. Otto, B., Österle, H.: Corporate Data Quality: Prerequisite for Successful Business Models. Springer Gabler, Berlin (2016)
3. Pipino, L., Wang, R., Kopcso, D., Rybolt, W.: Developing measurement scales for data-quality dimensions. Inf. Qual. **1**, 37–52 (2005)
4. Batini, C., Scannapieco, M.: Data and Information Quality: Concepts, Methodologies and Techniques. Springer, Cham (2016)
5. Batista, M.C.M.: Schema quality analysis in a data integration system. Ph.D. thesis, Universidade Federal de Pernambuco (2008)
6. Vossen, G.: Datenmodelle, Datenbanksprachen und Datenbankmanagementsysteme [Data Models, Database Languages, and Database Management Systems]. Oldenbourg Verlag (2008)
7. Heinrich, B., Hristova, D., Klier, M., Schiller, A., Szubartowicz, M.: Requirements for data quality metrics. J. Data Inf. Qual. **9**(2), 12:1–12:32 (2018)
8. Ehrlinger, L., Werth, B., Wöß, W.: QuaIIe: a data quality assessment tool for integrated information systems. In: Proceedings of the Tenth International Conference on Advances in Databases, Knowledge, and Data Applications (DBKDA 2018), pp. 21–31 (2018)
9. Euzenat, J., Shvaiko, P.: Ontology Matching. Springer, Secaucus (2007)
10. Batista, M.C.M., Salgado, A.C.: Information quality measurement in data integration schemas. In: Proceedings of the Fifth International Workshop on Quality in Databases, QDB 2007, at the VLDB 2007 Conference, pp. 61–72. ACM (2007)
11. Fenton, N., Bieman, J.: Software Metrics: A Rigorous and Practical Approach, 3rd edn. CRC Press, Boca Raton (2014)
12. Jain, A.K., Murty, M.N., Flynn, P.J.: Data clustering: a review. ACM Comput. Surv. (CSUR) **31**(3), 264–323 (2000)

13. Batista, M.C.M., Salgado, A.C.: Minimality quality criterion evaluation for integrated schemas. In: Second IEEE International Conference on Digital Information Management (ICDIM), pp. 436–441, December 2007
14. Batista, M.C.M., Salgado, A.C.: Data integration schema analysis: an approach with information quality. In: Proceedings of the 12th International Conference on Information Quality, pp. 447–461. MIT, Cambridge, November 2007
15. Duchateau, F., Bellahsene, Z.: Measuring the quality of an integrated schema. In: Parsons, J., Saeki, M., Shoval, P., Woo, C., Wand, Y. (eds.) ER 2010. LNCS, vol. 6412, pp. 261–273. Springer, Heidelberg (2010). https://doi.org/10.1007/978-3-642-16373-9_19
16. Ehrlinger, L., Wöß, W.: Semi-automatically generated hybrid ontologies for information integration. In: Joint Proceedings of the Posters and Demos Track of 11th International Conference on Semantic Systems - SEMANTiCS2015 and 1st Workshop on Data Science: Methods, Technology and Applications (DSci15), pp. 100–104. CEUR Workshop Proceedings (2015)
17. Ehrlinger, L., Wöß, W.: Automated schema quality measurement in large-scale information systems. In: Hacid, H., Sheng, Q.Z., Yoshida, T., Sarkheyli, A., Zhou, R. (eds.) WISE 2018. LNCS, vol. 10042, pp. 16–31. Springer, Cham (2019)
18. Wand, Y., Wang, R.Y.: Anchoring data quality dimensions in ontological foundations. Commun. ACM 39(11), 86–95 (1996)
19. Piro, A. (ed.): Informationsqualitt bewerten - Grundlagen, Methoden, Praxisbeispiele [Assessing Information Quality - Foundations, Methods, and Practical Examples], 1st edn. Symposion Publishing GmbH, Düsseldorf (2014)
20. Myers, D.: List of Conformed Dimensions of Data Quality (2017). http://dimensionsofdataquality.com/alldimensions. Accessed Dec 2018
21. Standard for a Software Quality Metrics Methodology. IEEE 1061-1998, Institute of Electrical and Electronics Engineers (1998)
22. Hinrichs, H.: Datenqualitätsmanagement in Data Warehouse-Systemen [Data Quality Management in Data Warehouse-Systems]. Ph.D. thesis, Universität Oldenburg (2002)
23. International Organization of Standardization: ISO/IEC 25012. https://iso25000.com/index.php/en/iso-25000-standards/iso-25012. Accessed Dec 2018
24. Pipino, L.L., Lee, Y.W., Wang, R.Y.: Data quality assessment. Commun. ACM 45(4), 211–218 (2002)
25. Loshin, D.: The Practitioner's Guide to Data Quality Improvement. Elsevier, Amsterdam (2010)
26. English, L.P.: Improving Data Warehouse and Business Information Quality: Methods for Reducing Costs and Increasing Profits. Wiley, Hoboken (1999)
27. Jarke, M., Lenzerini, M., Vassiliou, Y., Vassiliadis, P.: Fundamentals of Data Warehouses. Springer, Heidelberg (2000). https://doi.org/10.1007/978-3-662-05153-5
28. Cykana, P., Paul, A., Stern, M.: DoD guidelines on data quality management. In: Proceedings of the International Conference on Information Quality (MITICIQ), pp. 154–171 (1996)
29. Askham, N., et al.: The six primary dimensions for data quality assessment. Technical report, DAMA UK Working Group (2013)
30. Aggarwal, C.C.: Data Mining. Springer, Cham (2015). https://doi.org/10.1007/978-3-319-14142-8

# Automated Schema Quality Measurement in Large-Scale Information Systems

Lisa Ehrlinger[1,2(✉)] and Wolfram Wöß[1]

[1] Johannes Kepler University Linz, Linz, Austria
{lisa.ehrlinger,wolfram.woess}@jku.at
[2] Software Competence Center Hagenberg, Hagenberg im Mühlkreis, Austria
lisa.ehrlinger@scch.at

**Abstract.** Assessing the quality of information system schemas is crucial, because an unoptimized or erroneous schema design has a strong impact on the quality of the stored data, e.g., it may lead to inconsistencies and anomalies at the data-level. Even if the initial schema had an ideal design, changes during the life cycle can negatively affect the schema quality and have to be tackled. Especially in Big Data environments there are two major challenges: *large* schemas, where manual verification of schema and data quality is very arduous, and the integration of *heterogeneous* schemas from different data models, whose quality cannot be compared directly. Thus, we present a domain-independent approach for automatically measuring the quality of large and heterogeneous (logical) schemas. In contrast to existing approaches, we provide a fully automatable workflow that also enables regular reassessment. Our implementation allows to measure the quality dimensions correctness, completeness, pertinence, minimality, readability, and normalization.

## 1 Introduction

The trustworthiness of data-driven decisions (e.g., for artificial intelligence or enterprise strategies) depends directly on the quality of the underlying data. Poor data quality (DQ) leads to effects like cost increase, customer dissatisfaction, and organizational mistrust [1], which is why DQ has become critical for operational excellence [2]. According to Gartner Research [3], the average financial impact of poor data on businesses is $9.7 million per year.

Data quality is usually characterized by different *dimensions* [4], which can either refer to the *extension* of the data (i.e., data values), or to their *intension* (i.e., the schema) [5]. An information system (IS) schema describes the data structure and its relationships [6] and can also be denoted as *metadata*. While the majority of research into DQ focuses on the data values [5,7], this paper contributes to the less intensively researched but complementary topic of schema quality. Schema quality is essential for IS development, since an erroneous schema design strongly impacts the quality of an IS and its data values [5,7]. Redundancies at schema-level, for example, may lead to inconsistencies and anomalies

© Springer Nature Switzerland AG 2019
H. Hacid et al. (Eds.): QUAT 2018, LNCS 11235, pp. 16–31, 2019.
https://doi.org/10.1007/978-3-030-19143-6_2

at the data-level. The practical importance of automated schema quality measurement is also supported by Coelho et al. [8], who attested an unexpectedly poor quality to the majority of database (DB) schemas observed in their study on open-source software projects. In contrast to approaches that measure the quality of conceptual schemas, we focus on machine-readable logical schemas in order to investigate productive (and possibly legacy) information systems.

Our contribution is an approach for automated schema quality assessment, which addresses the following two challenges: (a) *large schemas*, where manual quality assessment is arduous, and the integration of (b) *heterogeneous schemas*, where a direct comparison of the quality is not possible, e.g., to decide which schema provides better DQ for a given query. We address challenge (a) with an automated approach and challenge (b) by establishing a mapping from the original IS schema to a standardized machine-readable schema description, which is explained in more detail in Sect. 3.1. The approach comprises three steps: (1) the mapping of an IS schema to a standardized representation, (2) similarity calculation between schema elements to detect overlappings and potential redundancies, and (3) the computation of quality metrics.

The quality measurement in its current implementation comprises metrics for the dimensions correctness, completeness, pertinence, minimality, readability, and normalization. Although schema quality metrics are usually based on similarity calculation (e.g., to determine if a schema element corresponds to its reference), details about this aspect are often left unclear [5]. For example, in [9], a schema must include predefined mappings that indicate similar or equal elements in order to be investigated. In contrast to existing approaches, this paper provides details of both quality and similarity calculation, which reveals new insights in the mutual dependency between the topics. We have implemented our approach in the DQ tool QualIe [10] in order to demonstrate its applicability.

A typical use case for our approach is quality measurement of schemas in a productive integrated information system. Such a system contains current as well as legacy data from IS represented by different data models. In many cases, no domain expert might be available for manual verification. An evaluation of the DQ and thus a measurement of the quality of the decisions derived from the data is hardly possible. Our approach allows to calculate a standard quality report for such IS schemas, which highlights the most important schema quality issues and provides a starting point for deeper investigation by a domain expert.

The remainder of this paper is structured as follows: Sect. 2 presents related research into schema quality measurement and schema matching. Section 3 covers the concept of our approach to measure the quality of large-scale and heterogeneous schemas and Sect. 4 its implementation followed by an evaluation and discussion.

## 2    Related Work

Generally, there is little research on schema quality measurement [5,7]. In contrast to manual approaches, such as [11] by Herden, the focus of this work is on automation. Related work in [7,8] is specifically attributed to relational DBs, whereas we consider heterogeneous schema models. Coelho et al. [8] observed mainly DB-specific quality issues of MySQL and PostgreSQL DBs. Kruse [7] studied the schema quality dimensions conciseness and normalization from the viewpoint of the data, including a detailed discussion on functional dependency discovery. Although our work has been developed from the viewpoint of the schema (in contrast to the data values), [7] is a valuable extension to the normalization dimension in Sect. 3.3.

Batista and Salgado [9] proposed an approach to measure and enhance the quality of schemas in an integrated IS by calculating the three quality dimensions completeness, minimality, and type consistency. There are two major differences compared to our work: (1) Batista and Salgado assume that their schemas are provided in XML format and include predefined mappings to indicate redundant attributes, and (2) they suggest a process for eliminating redundant elements from the schemas. Since our goal is the ad-hoc measurement of the quality of different schemas in productive use, the DQ tool itself must be able to handle data model heterogeneity and to generate mappings between them (i.e., carry out similarity calculation). Further, automatic quality enhancement was outside the scope of our work, since in productive systems this must usually be verified by an expert. In addition, Duchateau and Bellahense [12] presented an approach to measure the quality (including completeness, minimality, and structurality of schemas) of schema matching results compared to an expert-generated reference schema. In contrast, we assume sufficient quality of the selected schema matching approach and aim at the quality measurement of the schema itself.

After an initial harmonization step, the schemas in our work can be represented with an ontological description (cf. Sect. 3.1). Thus, in terms of schema matching, we focus on ontology matching, since ontologies have the highest semantic expressiveness among all schema representations [13]. A comprehensive classification of ontology matching is provided in [14]. The most commonly used matching methods are iterative similarity propagation, like the similarity flooding (SF) algorithm introduced in [15], as well as string-based approaches [14]. A particular feature of the SF algorithm is that no semantic information about the schema elements is required because the similarity calculation relies solely on the initial similarity values and the graph structure [15]. The DQ tool QuaIIe [10], where we implemented our approach, offers two different algorithms for schema similarity calculation: the SF algorithm and a customized similarity calculation for the machine-readable schema descriptions, which is further described in Sect. 3.2. Since the SF algorithm is a general applicable approach that delivers reasonable results for a vast variety of different scenarios [15], we used it as baseline to demonstrate the efficacy our similarity calculation.

# 3    An Approach to Schema Quality Measurement

This section introduces our high-level approach to measure the quality of large and different heterogeneous schemas with the aim to support a user (e.g., an IS architect) in the interpretation and enhancement of schema quality. The approach consists of three steps:

1. the mapping of an IS schema to a standardized representation,
2. similarity calculation between schema elements to detect overlappings and potential redundancies, and
3. the computation of quality metrics, based on features from the standardized schema representations as well as the original ISs including their content.

Quality measures can be annotated to the schema description for further analysis and reporting. The three steps are described in the following paragraphs.

## 3.1    Schema Harmonization

The harmonization step guarantees the comparability of heterogeneous schemas by providing a standardized machine-readable ontological description of each analyzed schema. Schema descriptions are represented by the DSD (data source description) vocabulary, which is based on the W3C Standard OWL[1] (Web Ontology Language). The mapping from different data models and details of DSD are provided in [16]. This mapping is a prerequisite to perform cross-schema calculations and to obtain information about a schema's similarity to other schemas. The most important terms of the DSD vocabulary used in this paper are:

- A dsd:Datasource $s$ represents one IS schema and has a type (e.g., relational database, spreadsheet) and an arbitrary number of concepts and associations, which are also referred to as "schema elements".
- A dsd:Concept $c$ is a real-world object and is usually equivalent to a table in a relational database (DB) or a class in an object-oriented DB.
- A dsd:Association $r$ is a relationship between two or more concepts.
- A dsd:Attribute $a$ is a property of a concept or an association; e.g., the column "first_name" provides information about the concept "employees".
- Primary keys $pk$ and foreign keys $fk$ represent key relationships in relational data.

The description of a schema $s$ is a directed, labeled graph that contains concepts, attributes, associations, and optionally constraints. A corresponding reference schema is denoted by $s'$ and comprises the corresponding reference elements $c'$, $a'$, and $r'$. Listing 1.1 shows the transformation of the two tables employees {emp_no: int, name: string, birth_date: date} and dept_emp {emp_no: int, dept_no: int} from a relational DB to a graph representation

---

[1] https://www.w3.org/OWL [December, 2018].

using the DSD vocabulary in Turtle[2] syntax. The additional table `departments`, as well as the attribute and primary key descriptions, which would also belong to the DSD description, are omitted for brevity. The example shows that a relational table can be transformed into a `dsd:Concept` or a `dsd:Association`. While the table `employees` is transformed to a concept since it represents persons, the table `dept_emp` is represented as `dsd:ReferenceAssociation` (a special association type) since it models the assignment of an employee to a department.

**Listing 1.1.** Example DSD File

```
1  ex: employees a dsd:Concept;
2    rdfs:label "employees";
3    dsd:hasPrimaryKey ex:employees.pk;
4    dsd:hasAttribute ex:employees.emp_no, ex:employees.name, ex:
        ↪ employees.birth_date.
5
6  ex:dept_emp a dsd:ReferenceAssociation;
7    rdfs:label "dept_emp";
8    dsd:hasPrimaryKey ex:dept_emp.pk;
9    dsd:hasAttribute ex:dept_emp.emp_no, ex:dept_emp.dept_no;
10   dsd:referencesTo ex:employees, ex:departments;
11   dsd:referencesTo ex:employees, ex:departments.
```

While this harmonization step enables comparability and quality measurement of schemas from different data models, it does not guarantee access to the original IS' content. Consequently, the metrics proposed in Sect. 3.3 primarily use the IS metadata instead of the content. An exception is the determination of the normal form, which is impossible without considering the semantics of the attributes that are derived from the content.

## 3.2   Schema Similarity Calculation

An essential prerequisite for the calculation of most schema quality metrics is the determination of equal or similar elements. Such information is vital to detect redundancies in one single schema or to determine whether a schema corresponds to a reference schema. Similarity calculation in schemas has been widely researched under the term *schema matching*, where the objective is automatic detection of correspondences (i.e., schema mappings) between schema elements to make statements about their similarity [14]. Automatic correspondence detection is usually based on a measure of similarity. In the context of this paper, a similarity $\sigma : e \times e \rightarrow \mathbb{R} \in [0,1]$ is a function that expresses the similarity between two elements by a real number that is normalized to $[0,1]$, where 1.0 denotes a perfect match and 0.0 complete dissimilarity [17]. In order to distinguish between identical, similar, and completely different elements, a threshold $t$

---

[2] https://www.w3.org/TR/turtle [December, 2018].

can be defined. Logan et al. [18] distinguish between four cases when comparing a data set (here: schema $s$) to its reference $s'$:

- *Correct elements (C):* the number of elements that correspond exactly to an element from the reference schema (i.e., have a similarity value of 1.0).
- *Incorrect elements (I):* the number of elements that have a similar element in the reference schema, but are not identical (i.e., $\sigma > t \wedge \sigma < 1.0$).
- *Missing elements (M):* the number of elements that exist in the reference schema, but have no correspondence in the schema under investigation.
- *Extra elements (E):* the number of elements that exist in the investigated schema, but have no corresponding element in the reference schema.

A common feature of all schemas used in the course of this work is that they rely on domain knowledge expressed with the DSD vocabulary. Thus, we developed a schema matching approach referred to as *DSD similarity*, which uses information contained in DSD files. In its most elementary form (i.e., without additional information like constraints), the graph-based structure of a DSD schema description can be reduced to a tree with three depth-levels: (1) the root node, i.e., the data source itself, (2) concepts and associations within the schema, and (3) attributes of concepts or associations at the third level. The calculation follows a bottom-up approach, because in order to calculate the similarity between two schemas, it is necessary to know the similarity between all schema elements (i.e., *concept and association similarity*). Further, the similarity calculation between schema elements depends on the similarity of their attributes (i.e., *attribute similarity*) and additional features (the label).

Consequently, each DSD element is characterized by a feature vector $v$, which is shown in Table 1. For example, an attribute is described by its label, its data type (e.g., string or integer) and three boolean features that declare if the attribute is unique, nullable, and incrementable. Each feature is compared to its corresponding feature in the reference element with an appropriate similarity measure. The symbol $f_1 \prec f_2$ indicates that $f_1$ is a subtype of $f_2$ (e.g., int $\prec$ numeric), which can be verified in Java using f1.isAssignableFrom(f2).

Although concepts and associations are, due to their semantic meanings, two different classes in DSD, both can consist of attributes, and in some cases it can not be determined whether an element from an original IS (e.g., a table in a relational DB) is a concept or an association. Thus, not only concept-concept and association-association, but also concept-association comparison is necessary.

The similarity calculation between two DSD elements is a parallel, non-weighted combination of different elementary matching techniques [14]. The aggregated similarity value between two DSD elements is then calculated using the Jaccard coefficient, that is, the ratio between the number of shared features and the unique number of features present in both elements [14]:

$$\sigma(v_1, v_2) = \frac{|v_1 \cap v_2|}{|v_1 \cup v_2|}. \tag{1}$$

**Table 1.** Feature vectors for DSD similarity

| Element | Feature | Similarity measure |
|---|---|---|
| Attribute | Label | String measure (Levensthein distance) |
| | Data type | $\sigma(f_1, f_2) = \begin{cases} 1.0 & \text{if } f_1 == f_2; \\ 0.5 & \text{if } f_1 \prec f_2 \vee f_2 \prec f_1; \\ 0.0 & \text{otherwise.} \end{cases}$ |
| | Boolean features (nullable, incrementable, unique) | $\sigma(f_1, f_2) = \begin{cases} 1.0 & \text{if } f_1 == f_2; \\ 0.0 & \text{otherwise.} \end{cases}$ |
| Concept + Association | Label | String measure (Levensthein distance) |
| | Attributes | Attribute similarity |
| | Data type | cf. attribute data type measure |
| Association | Connected concepts | Concept similarity |
| | Boolean features (disjointness, completeness) | cf. attribute boolean features |
| Schema | Concepts, associations | Concept and association similarity |

We demonstrate the application of this formula by calculating the similarity between concept employees ($v_1$) and the association dept_emp ($v_2$) from Listing 1.1. The two feature vectors $v_1$ and $v_2$ are composed out of seven distinct features: label, data type, and five attributes:

- $v_1$ { "employees", dsd:Concept, emp_no, name, birth_date }
- $v_2$ { "dept_emp", dsd:ReferenceAssociation, emp_no, dept_no }

The string similarity between the labels is with 0.4117 below the standard threshold (0.78) and the data type comparison yields 0.0 since dsd:Concept and dsd:ReferenceAssociation are different and have no subtype-relationship. The *attribute similarity* detects one shared feature (emp_no), which is why the similarity calculation yields a value of $1/7 = 0.1429$. Further details about the determination of the standard thresholds are described in Sect. 4.

## 3.3 Schema Quality Measurement

While many different schema quality dimensions exist, we have currently implemented metrics for correctness, completeness, pertinence, minimality, readability, and normalization. The following paragraphs give an overview on all six dimensions, where completeness, correctness, and pertinence require comparison against a reference schema. In practice, the reference could be the complete schema of an IIS (cf. [19]), a second schema to determine differences, or the investigated schema itself before and after modifications to ensure that defined quality parameters remain stable.

**Completeness.** Schema completeness describes the extent to which real-world concepts of the application domain and their attributes and relationships are represented in the schema [5]. We implemented the completeness metric by Logan et al. [18], who distinguish between correct (C), incorrect (I), extra (E) and missing (M) elements after a data set (here schema) is compared to its reference:

$$Com(s, s') = \frac{C + I}{C + I + M}. \tag{2}$$

**Correctness.** A database schema is considered correct if it corresponds to the real-world it is supposed to model [5]. It can be distinguished between correctness with respect to the model and with respect to requirements. We use the calculation presented by Logan et al. [18]:

$$Cor(s, s') = \frac{C}{C + I + E}. \tag{3}$$

**Pertinence.** Pertinence describes a schema's relevance, which means that a schema with low pertinence has a high number of unnecessary elements [5]. A schema that is perfectly complete and pertinent represents exactly the reference schema (i.e., its real world representation), which means that the two dimensions complement each other. Since no metric for schema pertinence exists in literature, we derived a new metric that is based on the formulas for correctness and completeness in [18]:

$$Per(s, s') = \frac{C + I}{C + I + E}. \tag{4}$$

**Normalization.** Normal forms (NFs) can be used to measure the quality of relations in a relational DB, in order to obtain a schema that avoids redundancies and resulting inconsistencies as well as insert, update, and delete anomalies [6]. Although this quality dimension refers to relational data, it is included in this work, because relational DBs predominate in enterprises. In our implementation, the second, third, and Boyce Codd normal form (2NF, 3NF, and BCNF, respectively) can be determined for both concepts and associations. Note that more time-efficient ways for the detection of functional dependencies exist, cf. [7].

**Readability.** A schema should be readable, which means it should represent the modeled domain in a natural and clear way so it is self-explanatory to the user [6]. Good readability supports the semantic expressiveness of a schema and enables automatic mappings to other domains that are based on dictionary approaches. However, poor readability in a logical IS schema (e.g., an attribute named `attr1`) has little impact on the quality of the IS content, in comparison to the other schema quality dimensions like minimality or completeness. The current version of our implementation does not include a calculator for the readability dimension, but its development is part of our ongoing research.

**Minimality.** A schema is defined as minimal if no parts of it can be omitted without loosing information, i.e., the schema is without redundancies [5]. This quality dimension is of particular interest in the context of IIS, where redundant representations are common. We developed a metric that is based on hierarchical clustering (to detect similar elements), where the number of clusters $|c|$ is divided by the number of elements $|e|$:

$$Min(s) = \begin{cases} 1.0, & \text{if } |e| = 1 \\ \frac{|c|-1}{|e|-1}, & \text{else.} \end{cases} \tag{5}$$

In order to produce results that are normalized to $[0, 1]$, the metric is shifted by $-1$, because in the case where all elements are completely redundant, $|c|$ yields a (minimum) value of 1. Consequently, Eq. 5 is normalized and interval-scaled according to the requirements for DQ metrics by Heinrich et al. [20]. A detailed discussion and proof of this metric is out of scope and published in [21].

### 3.4   Schema Quality Aggregation and Persistence

To persist and reuse schema quality measurements, we introduce an extension to the DSD vocabulary that allows quality aspects to be included in the DSD schema descriptions. We distinguish between two types of information that can be used to describe an element's quality: *quality ratings* and *quality annotations*. A quality rating (dsd:QualityRating) is a double value between 0 and 1 and is calculated with a quality metric, uniquely assigned to a specific dimension. This structure ensures on the one hand the comparability between quality ratings of different schemas, and on the other hand the explicit assignment of ratings to the same metric and dimension. Since a quality metric must be uniquely assigned to one dimension, it cannot contribute to multiple quality dimensions. Quality annotations (dsd:QualityAnnotation) provide additional information about an element's quality and are independent of any data type (e.g., a concept's FDs or NF). Annotations do not require a metric, but can be directly assigned to a dsd:QualityDimension to classify them at a higher level (e.g., FDs to normalization). The W3C developed the "Data Quality Vocabulary" [22] in parallel to our research, which is very similar to the DQ extension of the DSD vocabulary. We intend to evaluate the Data Quality Vocabulary for its suitability to use it in conjunction with the DSD vocabulary in the future.

Listing 1.2 shows the concept ex:employees from Listing 1.1, being described by an annotation with the value "BCNF" and a completeness rating of 0.85. This demonstrates the relationship between metrics, dimensions, and ratings in DSD.

**Listing 1.2.** Formalized DSD Quality Extension Example

```
1  ex:employees a dsd:Concept;
2    dsd:hasQuality ex:employees_quality.
3
4  ex:employees_quality a dsd:Quality;
5    dsd:hasAnnotation ex:qa01;
```

```
 6    dsd:hasRating ex:qr01.
 7
 8  ex:qa01 a dsd:QualityAnnotation;
 9    owl:hasValue "BCNF";
10    dsd:belongsToDimension dsd:NormalForm.
11
12  ex:qr01 a dsd:QualityRating;
13    owl:hasValue 0.85;
14    dsd:hasMetric dsd:RatioCompleteness;
15    dsd:measuredAt "2018-06-24".
16
17  dsd:NormalForm a dsd:QualityDimension.
18  dsd:Completeness a dsd:QualityDimension.
19  dsd:RatioCompleteness a dsd:QualityMetric;
20    owl:belongsToDimension dsd:Completeness.
```

## 4    Application and Discussion

To demonstrate the applicability of our approach, we have implemented it as part of QualIe (Quality Assessment for Integrated Information Environments, pronounced ['kvɑlə]), a Java-based tool to measure data and schema quality [10]. From a high-level view, QualIe consists of three components: (a) data source connectors, (b) quality calculators and (c) quality reporters. A connector sets up access to an IS and maps its elements to DSD elements. For each DQ dimension described in this paper there exists one DQ calculator that stores the results in form of quality ratings and annotations to the corresponding DSD elements. Two algorithms have been implemented to perform similarity calculation: DSD similarity and the SF algorithm proposed in [15]. Finally, the quality measurements can be exported as machine- and human-readable report or they can be continuously stored in a DB (to observe how quality evolves over time).

Recently, a call for more empiricism in DQ research has been proposed in [23], promoting both, (1) the evaluation on synthetic data sets to show the reproducibility of the measurements, and (2) evaluations on large real-world data to prove extended applicability. In this paper, we tackle both approaches. Thus, we selected the following DBs for the demonstration: (1) the employees[3] DB with six tables that contain about three million records, (2) Sakila[4] DB with 16 tables for the administration of a film distribution, (3) a relational sample DB for digital media called "Chinook"[5], (4) the well-known Northwind DB[6], (5) real-world stock exchange data collected from the Alphavantage API[7] called "alphavantage", and (6) a productive Cassandra DB called "metadynea" that

---

[3] https://dev.mysql.com/doc/employee/en [December, 2018].
[4] https://dev.mysql.com/doc/sakila/en [December, 2018].
[5] https://archive.codeplex.com/?p=chinookdatabase [December, 2018].
[6] https://docs.microsoft.com/en-us/dotnet/framework/data/adonet/sql/linq/ downloading-sample-databases [December, 2018].
[7] https://www.alphavantage.co [December, 2018].

stores about 60 GB of chemometrics data on three nodes. Our aim was to use both, well-known synthetic data sets as well as large real world data sets for the evaluation of DQ measurements. We selected the employees schema due to a special case, where the parallel associations dept_emp and dept_manager model two semantically different roles between the same entity types. Although there is no semantic redundancy, the two relations have a high similarity and are suited to demonstrate our minimality metric.

To promote the reconstruction of the quality calculations performed in this demonstration, we published an executable (QualIe.jar) and DSD files for the employed DB schemas on our project website[8]. The program takes one mandatory and one optional command line parameter: (1) the path to the DSD schema to be observed and (2) the path to the reference schema. In addition to the minimality calculation discussed in the following paragraphs, the demo program performs schema quality calculations for the dimensions completeness, correctness, and pertinence, and provides the results in form of a XML quality report.

### 4.1   Schema Similarity Calculation and Parameter Selection

Calculating DSD similarity requires appropriate thresholds and string distances to be selected. This section evaluates a variety of parameter settings to support optimal results and provide a best-practice recommendation. Of course, a different parameter selection might yield better results in specific application domains. There are four parameters that can be selected by a user: (1) the type of string similarity, (2) a threshold for the string similarity $t_{ss}$, (3) a threshold for the attribute similarity $t_{as}$, and (4) a threshold for the recursively computed concept similarity in associations $t_{cs}$. We evaluated seven parameters for the thresholds: 0.78, 0.8, 0.82, 0.85, 0.9, 0.95, and 1.0. In the test scenario, the employees DB schema was compared to itself to verify that the similarity matrix yields mirrored results. This is important to ensure that two schema elements achieve the same similarity value independently in which order they are compared to each other (i.e., $\sigma(e_1, e_2) = \sigma(e_2, e_1)$). This basic evaluation also indicates whether an element always achieves a similarity of 1.0 to itself.

In the DSD representation of the employees schema, the tables dept_emp and dept_manager were represented as reference associations, whereas the other four were represented as concepts. For each of the 686 parameter setting combinations, a similarity matrix was calculated and compared against a perfect reference similarity matrix, which was created manually by an expert. We calculated the Mean Squared Error

$$MSE = \frac{1}{n * m} \sum_{i=1}^{n*m} (\sigma_i - \sigma'_i)^2 \tag{6}$$

for each parameter combination, where $n$ is the number of columns and $m$ the number of rows in the similarity matrix, which resulted in $n * m$ calculated $\sigma$ values that were compared to their corresponding values in the reference matrix.

---

[8] http://dqm.faw.jku.at [December, 2018].

The results show a strong influence of the attribute similarity threshold $t_{as}$ and a very weak influence of the concept similarity threshold $t_{cs}$, because the employees schema contains only two associations and concept similarity forms only part of the association similarity. The parameter combination with the lowest MSE of 0.0102 yields the similarity matrix in Table 2. These parameters are consequently used as "standard parameters" for our evaluations:

- String similarity: Levenshtein distance
- String similarity threshold $t_{ss}$: 0.78
- Attribute similarity threshold $t_{as}$: 0.9
- Concept similarity threshold $t_{cs}$: 0.9.

**Table 2.** Similarity matrix for employees schema

|               | departments | dept_emp | dept_manager | employees | salaries | titles |
|---------------|-------------|----------|--------------|-----------|----------|--------|
| departments   | 1.0         | 0.125    | 0.125        | 0.1       | 0.125    | 0.125  |
| dept_emp      | 0.125       | 1.0      | 0.875        | 0.1818    | 0.2222   | 0.1    |
| dept_manager  | 0.125       | 0.875    | 1.0          | 0.1818    | 0.2222   | 0.1    |
| employees     | 0.1         | 0.1818   | 0.1818       | 1.0       | 0.1818   | 0.1818 |
| salaries      | 0.125       | 0.2222   | 0.2222       | 0.1818    | 1.0      | 0.375  |
| titles        | 0.125       | 0.1      | 0.1          | 0.1818    | 0.375    | 1.0    |

We additionally compared the results of DSD similarity to the SF algorithm [15] using the standard SF parameters (initial similarity $\sigma^0$: 0.5; threshold: 0.05; max. iterations: 2,000). With this comparison, we also wanted to show that our schema quality approach is general enough to be used with different schema matching algorithms for the similarity calculation. We observed that the overall distribution of the similarity values of the SF algorithm closely resembles the results gathered with DSD similarity, and – most important – that the matrix is symmetric. However, the $\sigma$ values of SF were generally lower (e.g., 0.026 between dept_emp and titles), and identical concepts did not always achieve a similarity value of 1.0 (e.g., 0.7145 for departments). Having a MSE of 0.1148, the SF algorithm performed acceptable, but clearly inferior to DSD similarity with $t_{as} < 0.82$ and all other thresholds set to any tested value $< 1.0$. Therefore, the DSD similarity is more suited for subsequent DQ measurement in our approach since it is adjusted to the DSD structure. This finding aligns with the fact that the SF algorithm is a general applicable approach that does not aim at outperforming custom schema matchers [15].

## 4.2 Schema Quality Measurement

To demonstrate the applicability of our schema quality metrics, we show measurements results in Tables 3 and 4. In addition to the data source schemas introduced in Sect. 5, we employed three modified versions of the Sakila DB ($Sakila_{GS}$): one with minor modifications but without removing or adding elements to affect correctness ($Sakila_1$), a second one where attributes and tables have been removed to affect completeness ($Sakila_2$), and a third one where attributes and tables have been added to affect pertinence ($Sakila_3$). To assess the usability of the results, five IS experts rated the fulfillment of the dimensions for the respective IS schemas intuitively with a number between 1.0 (complete fulfillment) and 0.0 (not fulfilled at all) as well as a self-assessment regarding their expertise. We computed a "target measurement" for each dimension and schema, which is the weighted average of all expert's assessment, where the expertise was used as weight. The expert rating is displayed in the parentheses next to each measurement.

**Table 3.** Data quality measurements requiring a gold standard

| Schema | Correctness | Completeness | Pertinence |
|---|---|---|---|
| $Sakila_{GS}$ | 1.0 (1.0) | 1.0 (1.0) | 1.0 (1.0) |
| $Sakila_1$ | 0.813 (0.960) | 1.0 (1.0) | 1.00 (1.0) |
| $Sakila_2$ | 0.929 (0.900) | 0.813 (0.839) | 0.929 (1.0) |
| $Sakila_3$ | 0.824 (0.934) | 0.938 (1.0) | 0.882 (0.876) |

**Table 4.** Data quality measurements without gold standard

| Schema | Minimality | Normal form |
|---|---|---|
| Sakila | 1.0 (1.0) | 6 tables BCNF, 9 tables 2NF, 1 table 1NF |
| employees | 0.800 (0.973) | All tables BCNF |
| Chinook | 1.0 (1.0) | 6 tables BCNF, 5 tables 2NF |
| alphavantage | 1.0 (1.0) | 1 table BCNF |
| Northwind | 1.0 (1.0) | 6 tables BCNF, 4 tables 2NF, 1 table 1NF |
| metadynea | 0.667 (0.696) | Not applicable for Cassandra |

Generally, the DQ measurements reflect the expert perception quite well. However, we recognized that humans would not downgrade pertinence when elements have been deleted, or completeness, when elements have been added. In addition, correctness and minimality typically rate stricter than humans. For example, even the obviously normalized Cassandra schema "metadynea" has been rated higher by humans. Interestingly, the special case in the employees DB (dept_emp, dept_manager) was also recognized by two experts, but with far less impact. For the NF we only provided the results, because experts and implementation likewise provided the same results.

# 5    Conclusions

We described a holistic approach to measure the quality of large-scale and different heterogeneous IS schemas, considering metrics for the dimensions completeness, correctness, pertinence, minimality, readability, and normalization. While such metrics are often based on determining the similarity between elements, many approaches do not specify how similarity is in fact calculated in the course of schema quality measurement. However, the most fundamental challenge in this work was the mutual dependency of schema matching and schema quality measurement. Schema matching requires identical and similar elements to be identified in order to detect alignments between them. Such alignments between corresponding elements can be determined between two different schemas (e.g., the schema observed and its reference schema) or within one individual schema. In both cases, the quality of the match highly depends on the quality of the selected similarity calculation. On the one hand, the quality of the similarity calculation can be evaluated by means of data quality measurement. For instance, Batini et al. [24] suggested verifying the quality of matched schemas with completeness, correctness, minimality, and understandability. On the other hand, it is important to recognize that DQ measurement requires schema matching methods (and thus similarity calculation) to compute specific quality metrics. This interrelation must be considered to ensure that suitable algorithms are selected for schema quality measurement and that results are interpreted correctly.

Our future work focuses on (1) a visual representation of the data quality report, which—due to the complexity of the information contained—is not a trivial task, but is essential for practical applications, (2) assessing and implementing the readability dimension, and (3) implementing and verifying the quality measurement of data in NoSQL databases.

**Acknowledgments.** The research reported in this paper has been supported by the Austrian Ministry for Transport, Innovation and Technology, the Federal Ministry for Digital and Economic Affairs, and the Province of Upper Austria in the frame of the COMET center SCCH.

# References

1. Redman, T.C.: The impact of poor data quality on the typical enterprise. Commun. ACM **41**(2), 79–82 (1998)
2. Otto, B., Österle, H.: Corporate Data Quality: Prerequisite for Successful Business Models. Springer Gabler, Berlin (2016)
3. Moore, S.: How to Create a Business Case for Data Quality Improvement. Gartner Research (2017). http://www.gartner.com/smarterwithgartner/how-to-create-a-business-case-for-data-quality-improvement. Accessed Dec 2018
4. Wand, Y., Wang, R.Y.: Anchoring data quality dimensions in ontological foundations. Commun. ACM **39**(11), 86–95 (1996)
5. Batini, C., Scannapieco, M.: Data and Information Quality: Concepts, Methodologies and Techniques. Springer (2016)

6. Vossen, G.: Datenmodelle, Datenbanksprachen und Datenbankmanagementsysteme [Data Models, Database Languages, and Database Management Systems]. Oldenbourg Verlag (2008)
7. Kruse, S.: Scalable data profiling - distributed discovery and analysis of structural metadata. Ph.D. thesis, Universität Potsdam (2018)
8. Coelho, F., Aillos, A., Pilot, S., Valeev, S.: On the quality of relational database schemas in open-source software. Int. J. Adv. Softw. **4**(3 & 4), 11 (2012)
9. Batista, M.C.M., Salgado, A.C.: Information quality measurement in data integration schemas. In: Proceedings of the Fifth International Workshop on Quality in Databases, QDB 2007, at the VLDB 2007 Conference, pp. 61–72. ACM (2007)
10. Ehrlinger, L., Werth, B., Wöß, W.: QuaIIe: a data quality assessment tool for integrated information systems. In: Proceedings of the Tenth International Conference on Advances in Databases, Knowledge, and Data Applications (DBKDA 2018), pp. 21–31 (2018)
11. Herden, O.: Measuring quality of database schema by reviewing - concept, criteria and tool. In: Proceedings of 5th International Workshop on Quantitative Approaches in Object-Oriented Software Engineering, pp. 59–70 (2001)
12. Duchateau, F., Bellahsene, Z.: Measuring the quality of an integrated schema. In: Parsons, J., Saeki, M., Shoval, P., Woo, C., Wand, Y. (eds.) ER 2010. LNCS, vol. 6412, pp. 261–273. Springer, Heidelberg (2010). https://doi.org/10.1007/978-3-642-16373-9_19
13. Feilmayr, C., Wöß, W.: An analysis of ontologies and their success factors for application to business. Data Knowl. Eng. **101**, 1–23 (2016)
14. Euzenat, J., Shvaiko, P.: Ontology Matching. Springer-Verlag New York Inc., Secaucus (2007)
15. Melnik, S., Garcia-Molina, H., Rahm, E.: Similarity flooding: a versatile graph matching algorithm and its application to schema matching. In: Proceedings of the 18th International Conference on Data Engineering, ICDE 2002, pp. 117–128. IEEE Computer Society, Washington, DC (2002)
16. Ehrlinger, L., Wöß, W.: Semi-automatically generated hybrid ontologies for information integration. In: Joint Proceedings of the Posters and Demos Track of 11th International Conference on Semantic Systems, pp. 100–104. CEUR Workshop Proceedings (2015)
17. Cohen, W., Ravikumar, P., Fienberg, S.: A comparison of string metrics for matching names and records. In: KDD Workshop on Data Cleaning and Object Consolidation, vol. 3, pp. 73–78 (2003)
18. Logan, J.R., Gorman, P.N., Middleton, B.: Measuring the quality of medical records: a method for comparing completeness and correctness of clinical encounter data. In: American Medical Informatics Association Annual Symposium, AMIA 2001, Washington, DC, USA, 3–7 November 2001, pp. 408–4012 (2001)
19. Naumann, F., Freytag, J.C., Leser, U.: Completeness of integrated information sources. Inf. Syst. **29**(7), 583–615 (2004)
20. Heinrich, B., Hristova, D., Klier, M., Schiller, A., Szubartowicz, M.: Requirements for data quality metrics. J. Data Inf. Qual. **9**(2), 12:1–12:32 (2018)
21. Ehrlinger, L., Wöß, W.: A novel data quality metric for minimality. In: Hacid, H., Sheng, Q.Z., Yoshida, T., Sarkheyli, A., Zhou, R. (eds.) WISE 2018. LNCS, vol. 10042, pp. 1–15. Springer, Cham (2019)
22. W3C Working Group: Data on the Web Best Practices: Data Quality Vocabulary. (2016). https://www.w3.org/TR/vocab-dqv. Accessed Dec 2018

23. Sadiq, S., et al.: Data quality: the role of empiricism. ACM SIGMOD Rec. **46**(4), 35–43 (2018)
24. Batini, C., Lenzerini, M., Navathe, S.B.: A comparative analysis of methodologies for database schema integration. ACM Comput. Surv. **18**(4), 323–364 (1986)

# Email Importance Evaluation in Mailing List Discussions

Kun Jiang[1], Chunming Hu[1(✉)], Jie Sun[1], Qi Shen[1], and Xiaohan Jiang[2]

[1] Beijing Advanced Innovation Center for Big Data and Brain Computing,
Beihang University, Beijing 100191, China
{jiangkun,hucm,sunjie,shenqi}@act.buaa.edu.cn
[2] Beijing University of Technology, Beijing 100124, China
jxh@emails.bjut.edu.cn

**Abstract.** Nowadays, mailing lists are widely used in team work for discussion and consultation. Identifying important emails in mailing list discussions could significantly benefit content summary and opinion leader recognition. However, previous studies only focus on the importance evaluation methods regarding personal emails, and there is no consensus on the definition of important emails. Therefore, in this paper we consider the characteristics of mailing lists and study how to evaluate email importance in mailing list discussions. Our contribution mainly includes the following aspects. First, we propose ER-Match, an email conversation thread reconstruction algorithm that takes nested quotation relationships into consideration while constructing the email relationship network. Based on the email relationship network, we formulate the importance of emails in mailing list discussions. Second, we propose a feature-rich learning method to predict the importance of new emails. Furthermore, we characterize various factors affecting email importance in mailing list discussions. Experiments with publicly available mailing lists show that our prediction model outperforms baselines with large gains.

**Keywords:** Mailing list · Email thread reconstruction ·
Email importance modelling · Feature evaluation

## 1 Introduction

Mailing lists are widely used in team work to facilitate cooperation. They provide platforms for users to discuss, store and trace expertise. For example, about 3 million emails are archived in Linux kernel mailing list(LKML[1]) and we can learn kernel development and search specific issues about Linux kernel there. The World Wide Web Consortium(W3C) maintains hundreds of mailing lists[2] to foster a highly interactive community and promote the development of web standards.

---

[1] https://lkml.org.
[2] https://lists.w3.org/.

© Springer Nature Switzerland AG 2019
H. Hacid et al. (Eds.): QUAT 2018, LNCS 11235, pp. 32–45, 2019.
https://doi.org/10.1007/978-3-030-19143-6_3

Identifying important emails in mailing list discussions is significant. On one hand, extracting and summarizing important email information helps users to get main opinions of mailing list discussions. On the other hand, identifying important emails helps to recognize contributor. Generally speaking, people who send more important emails are supposed to be contributors or opinion leaders.

Previous studies only focus on the importance evaluation regarding personal emails [1,4,5,15,18,20]. It's worth noting that personal emails are used for point-to-point and point-to-multipoint communication, while mailing lists provide a platform where everyone subscribing the same mailing list will receive the same push emails. Unlike explicit relationships of personal mails, we can only figure out email relationships in mailing lists by quotation. Due to the more complex thread structure of emails in mailing lists, it's more meaningful to identify important emails. However, as far as we know, no previous exists on email importance evaluation in mailing list discussions.

In this paper, we extend existing personal email importance model into mailing lists. Previous studies usually use email user actions (e.g. replies, forwards) to evaluate email importance [1,4,15]. In consideration of the complex conversation structure of mailing list discussions, we add the quotation relationship into email importance modelling. In mailing lists, quotation is used to emphasize the context of opinions. Nested quotation relationships indicate more indirect relationships between emails, which helps us to disentangle email threads.

To get the relationships between emails, ER-Match, an email conversion thread reconstruction algorithm is proposed to build email relationship network. Based on the network model and our definition of important emails, we can directly rank emails in historical mailing list archives. Then we define important email and propose a learning method to predict important emails. With this prediction model, we can not only predict the importance value of new emails, but also get the insight on what features may contribute to the importance of emails in mailing list discussions through feature evaluation.

Our main contributions can be summarized as follows.

- We propose ER-Match, an email thread reconstruction algorithm, that can construct email relationship network. As far as we know, we are the first who consider email quotation relationships in email importance modelling.
- We propose a learning method to predict important emails in mailing list discussions. Experiments with publicly available mailing lists show that our prediction model outperforms baselines with large gains. And we get some interesting conclusions through feature evaluation.

The rest of the paper is organized as follows. We review the related work in Sect. 2. In Sect. 3, we define important email based on proposed network model. We detail a novel important email prediction model in Sect. 4. Then we evaluate this model and features based on data from real-world mailing lists in Sect. 5. Finally, we conclude this paper in Sect. 6.

## 2   Related Work

In this section we introduce existing researches on email thread reconstruction, which inspired us when building the mailing list conversation thread. Beyond that, some previous solutions for email importance evaluation are also discussed.

### 2.1   Email Thread Reconstruction

The way we build our network is similar to the solution of thread reconstruction problem. The main point of solving this kind of problem is setting an email conversation thread. This thread is a topic-centric discussion unit which contains exchanged emails within the same group [5]. Email thread reconstruction is a task of detecting conversation threads, and methods can be divided into two groups: metadata-based and content-based.

Metadata-based approaches mainly consider email metadata information. For example, the author of [19] proposes a message threading method based on in-reply-to and reference attributes of email header, and the method is applied to Netscape Mail. However, since email metadata are not available most of the time, content-based approaches are proposed to construct email threads.

Content-based methods can be divided into two categories, one of which is to get the correspondence between emails and threads. This approach is trying to obtain sequential liner structure among messages. Wu et al. [16] propose that after removal of any sequence of 're:', 'fw:', and 'fwd:' prefixes from subjects, emails with the same subject line are supposed to belong to the same conversation thread. A more recent study [14] tries to solve this problem through two-steps. They cluster emails with some clustering algorithm and then identify email threads using threading features such as sender and subject. Since these methods can't get the direct relationships between messages, some approaches are proposed to construct tree structure between emails according to reply relationships. Lewis et al. [9] convert the thread reconstruction problem into searching problem and propose 5 search strategies. Their experiment results show that the most effective strategy is to use email quotation as query and email content without quotation as search object. Joshi et al. [8] suppose that the contents of old emails exist as separate segments in reply emails and they try to construct tree structure by matching these segmentations.

Our approach refers to the search method of [8,9], but we additionally consider metadata and nested quotation relationships. The final data structure we use is a weighted directed graph, which provides new insights about how to get more contextual information for email data mining.

### 2.2   Email Importance

Existing researches on personal email importance can be divided into two different categories: sender-based and feature-based.

Sender-based approaches [6,15] mainly use trust scores of email senders. Golbeck et al. [6] propose TrustMail and it's a pioneering work using trust networks for email importance measurement. TrustMail prioritizes emails by inferring trust scores from senders. This approach supposes that emails from high trust score senders are more likely to be important. Besides, they assume transitivity, asymmetry, and personalization as most crucial properties of trust of their approach. Tsugawa et al. [15] extend the TrustMail and additionally take the trust scores of recipients into consideration. They called it EMIRT which stands for Estimating message importance from inter-recipient trust. However, these approaches only focus on senders or recipients' information while ignore other metadata of emails such as contents and send-time.

On the other hand, some previous studies [1,5,18,20] focus on feature-based methods. Aderdeen et al. [1] introduce the learning methods behind Gmail to evaluate new emails for better email triage. In this prediction model, four categories of features are proposed but not described in detail. Facing the problem of lack of annotation data, they suppose that importance ground truth is based on user action towards emails within a period of time. Zhang et al. [20] propose an email importance prediction system trained on manual annotated data, they only focus on features that can be extracted from text such as N-gram features, part-of-speech tags, length features and content features. But these approaches are used to solve personal email importance evaluation and don't consider the characteristics of mailing lists. Therefore, email importance evaluation in mailing list discussions is still a problem.

## 3   Email Importance Model

In this section, we propose a novel algorithm for constructing email relationship network. Moreover, we introduce our definition of important email. To construct the email importance model for mailing list discussions, we extend previous models of personal email importance evaluation by considering the indirect relationships between emails. To be specific, we take nested quotation into consideration and obtain the indirect relationships between emails in mailing list discussions.

### 3.1   Network Construction

Considering the fact that reply relationship itself is insufficient to represent email context, we therefore take nested quotation relationships into account when building email relationship network. We extend previous works [8,9] to obtain indirect relationships between emails.

Figure 1 illustrates that emails are quoted in two ways [13]: inline-reply and original-message. When emails are quoted in the way of inline-reply, we can get the nested quotation according to the identifier '>'. The number of identifiers represents the layer of nested quotation. For example, contents with '>' represent direct quotation and contents with identifier '>>' or '>>>' represent indirect quotation. For each email $E_i$ in email corpus, we set the quotation of $E_i$ as $EQ_i$ and $EQ_{ij}$ represents the j-th layer of nested quotation $EQ_i$. Morever, we can identify the original-message type by nested headers.

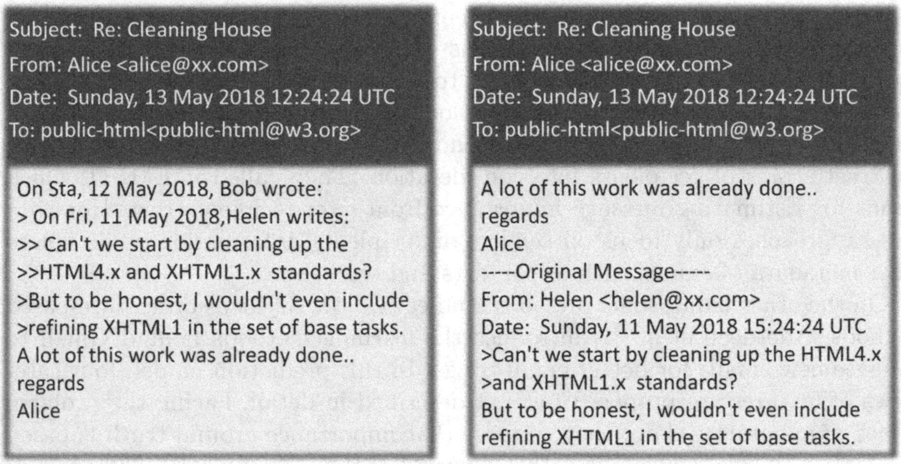
Subject: Re: Cleaning House
From: Alice <alice@xx.com>
Date: Sunday, 13 May 2018 12:24:24 UTC
To: public-html<public-html@w3.org>

On Sta, 12 May 2018, Bob wrote:
> On Fri, 11 May 2018,Helen writes:
>> Can't we start by cleaning up the
>>HTML4.x and XHTML1.x standards?
>But to be honest, I wouldn't even include
>refining XHTML1 in the set of base tasks.
A lot of this work was already done..
regards
Alice

Subject: Re: Cleaning House
From: Alice <alice@xx.com>
Date: Sunday, 13 May 2018 12:24:24 UTC
To: public-html<public-html@w3.org>

A lot of this work was already done..
regards
Alice
-----Original Message-----
From: Helen <helen@xx.com>
Date: Sunday, 11 May 2018 15:24:24 UTC
>Can't we start by cleaning up the HTML4.x
>and XHTML1.x standards?
But to be honest, I wouldn't even include
refining XHTML1 in the set of base tasks.

**Fig. 1.** Two types of quotation.

After quotation extraction, we convert quotation into bag of words. Then we match quoted messages in indexed emails by keyword matching. The relationship matching algorithm is shown in Algorithm 1.

According to [9], full quotation relationships are recognized as responses (replies or forwards). As for nested quotation, we need to traverse each layer of nested quotation to search the quoted emails. The weight of edges can be calculated according to the Definition 1. It is worth noting that an email might reply to a specific topic without any quotation. As for this case, we assume the email replies to the first email in its email conversation thread.

### 3.2 Important Email in Mailing Lists

To have a formal definition of important email is necessary before we can evaluate the importance of different emails. We divided this definition into two steps. Inspired by the definition of heterogeneous social network [10], we first define the email relationship network. Then we define important emails based on the network model.

**Definition 1 (Email Relationship Network).** *Email relationship network* $N = \{G1,\ G2,\ G3...\ \}$*, each G is a directed weighted graph, which represents an email conversation thread.* $G = <V,\ E>$ *where V is a set of vertices, representing emails and E is a set of edges, representing user actions. Given two nodes u,v in an email relationship network,* $\eta$ *is denoted as user action type and* $\eta \ \epsilon \ \{reply,\ forward,\ quotation\}$*.* $e_{uv}$ *represents the weight of the edge from u to v.* $e_{uv} = Quotation_{uv}/Quotation_u$ *where* $Quotation_{uv}$ *represents the content u quotes from v and* $Quotation_u$ *represents all the quotation of u. We can conclude that* $e_{uv} = 1$ *if* $\eta_{uv} \epsilon \{reply,\ forward\ \}$*.*

**Algorithm 1.** Match relationships(reply, forward, quotation) between emails

**Input:** emails E with their quotation EQ, The layer of nested quotation N
**Output:** the quotation of E quotationList, each quotation is represented as quotation(E, target, weight)

1: $w \leftarrow 1$
2: **for** $i = 0 \rightarrow E.length - 1$ **do**
3:    **if** $EQ_i$ is null **then**
4:       $quotedEmail = minTime(E|E.subject = Ei.subject)$
5:       $quotationList.add(quotation(E_i, quotedEmail, weight = w))$
6:       $break$
7:    **else**
8:       $quotedEmail = SEARCH(E_i, EQ_i)$
9:       $quotationList.add(quotation(E_i, quotedEmail, weight = w))$
10:       **for** $j = 1 \rightarrow N_i$ **do**
11:          $quotedEmail = SEARCH(E_i, EQ_{ij})$
12:          $w = wordcount(EQ_{ij})/wordcount(EQ_i)$
13:          $quotationList.add(quotation(E_i, quotedEmail, weight = w))$
14:       **end for**
15:    **end if**
16: **end for**
17: **return** $quotationList$

For example, in Fig. 2, the email relationship network consists of two conversation threads, while thread1 is composed of three emails a, b, c. We can conclude that c replies to b, b replies to a and c quotes a. $e_{cb} = 1, e_{ba} = 1$, $e_{ca} \approx 0.5$.

**Definition 2 (Importance Score).** *The importance score of a given node v is the sum of all in-edges weight. if $u \in E$ and $e_{uv} >= 0$, the importance score of v importance(v) can be get by the following equation:*

$$importance(v) = \sum e_{uv} \qquad (1)$$

Emails with more user actions are supposed to be more important. Therefore, we take both direct and indirect relationships between emails into consideration and we get the formula of email importance score. For example, we can get importance(a) $\approx 1.5$, importance(b) $= 1$, importance(c) $= 0$ from Fig. 2.

**Definition 3 (Important Email).** *Given a threshold t. Email e is important if importance(e) $> t$.*

According to our definition of importance score, we can evaluate email importance and rank emails in historical mailing list archives. To obtain the ground truth of prediction task, it's necessary to set a threshold to recognize important emails. When important email is defined, users can get important emails in conversation threads they have participated in, an example is shown in Fig. 3.

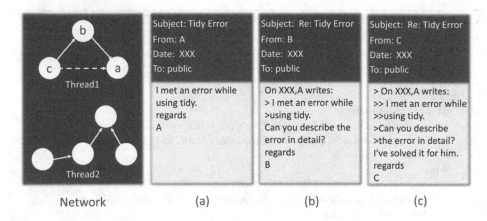

**Fig. 2.** Email relationship network example.

## 4    Important Email Prediction

When a new email adds into an email thread as a new node, the lack of inbound links often leads to a low importance score for the node. Therefore, we propose a learning method to predict the importance of new emails, which helps to optimize our email importance model. What's more, we can evaluate proposed features to study what makes an important email in the prediction model.

According to the definition of important emails in mailing lists, we have the annotated data of important and unimportant emails. The prediction model of important emails is transformed into a classification problem.

### 4.1    Feature Engineering

We propose some features extracted from time, contents, social interactions and thread structure in this subsection. Table 1 illustrates a specific description.

**Temporal Features.** According to [17], the most effective features that influence user reply-time towards emails in enterprises are temporal features. Therefore, we propose temporal feature group based on the send-time and we adjust all the time to UTC time zone due to the different time zone of senders.

**Content Features.** Research [20] shows that email importance is correlated with email content, so we extract features from email subject and body[3]. We use the open source project TextBlob[4] to get the polarity and subjectivity of subject and body content. Following work proposed in [2], we propose semanticDistance

---

[3] The body here refers to contents without header, signature and quotation.

[4] https://github.com/sloria/TextBlob.

**Table 1.** Feature list (e: the email).

| Feature group | Feature | Feature description |
|---|---|---|
| Temporal features | Interval | The reply interval of e |
| | TimeOfDay | The time of the day(0–6,6–12,12–18,18–24) |
| | TimeOfWeek | The day of the week(Sun, Mon...Sat) |
| | IsWeekend | Whether the day belongs to weekend |
| Content features | SubjectLength | The length of subject |
| | BodyLength | The length of body |
| | SemanticDistance | The semantic distance between e and the emails before e in the thread |
| | SubjectPolarity | The polarity of subject |
| | SubjectSubjectivity | The subjectivity of subject |
| | BodyPolarity | The polarity of body |
| | BodySubjectivity | The subjectivity of body |
| Thread features | CurrentEmailNum | The email number before e in the thread |
| | CurrentUserNum | The user number before e in the thread |
| Social features | HistoryInteractEmail | Historical quoted number per email for the sender of e |
| | HistoryInteractUser | Historical interact user number per thread for the sender of e |

---

**Algorithm 2.** Calculate the semanticDistance

---

**Input:** email corpus E without header, signature and quotation
**Output:** the semanticDistance SD of E
1: **for** $i = 0 \rightarrow E.length - 1$ **do**
2:     $preE \leftarrow$ the emails before $E_i$ in the same thread
3:     $preContent \leftarrow ""$
4:     **for** $j = 0 \rightarrow preE.length - 1$ **do**
5:         $preContent.append(preE_j)$
6:     **end for**
7:     $WV \leftarrow TFIDF.toWordVec(E_i)$
8:     $preWV \leftarrow TFIDF.toWordVec(preContent)$
9:     Convert WV and preWV into relative word vectors
10:     $SD_i = cosSimilarity(WV, preWV)$
11: **end for**
12: **return** $SD$

---

algorithm to calculate the similarity between a new email and all the emails in the conversation thread before. The semanticDistance algorithm is described in Algorithm 2.

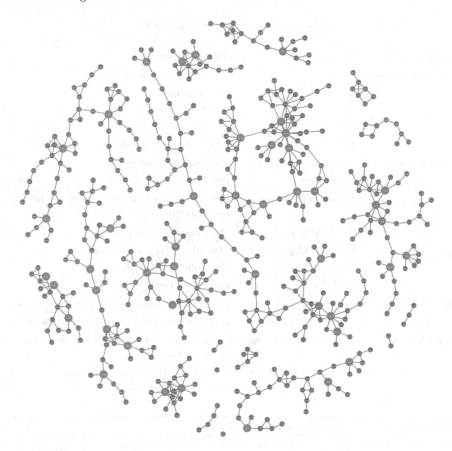

**Fig. 3.** A user's email relationship network and important emails (threshold = 2).

**Thread Features.** After building the email relationship network, we can extract some features from thread structure itself. The number of emails and users before new emails is considered. We assume that the more emails involved in discussions, the more likely people will participate in the discussions and new emails are more likely to have more responses. The feature group checks whether there is Matthew effect [11] in mailing list discussions.

**Social Features.** We propose this feature group to distinguish different senders. 'HistoryInteractEmail' represents each sender's historical importance score per email and 'HistoryInteractUser' represents each sender's historical interactive user number per thread.

### 4.2  Classification Model

In this paper, different classification models are used and compared. The ground truth is obtained according to the definition of important emails in Sect. 3.2.

We evaluate different classification algorithms such as LR, SVM and XGBoost [3] in our prediction model. Experiment result shows that XGBoost achieves the best performance. We use sklearn[5] package for the implementation of XGBoost. We find the optimal parameters of the model by cross validation and grid searching[6] [7].

# 5 Experiment

In this section, we compare the performance of our important email prediction model with some related work on 5 publicly available mailing lists. Besides, we also conduct a feature evaluation process to find out which features contribute more to the importance score of emails in mailing list discussions.

## 5.1 DataSet

The datasets we use are collected from W3C public mailing list archives. These mailing lists record the discussions during standard draft and revision. We combine five mailing lists into a total of 240,000 emails as our dataset. The five mailing lists are www-style, public-whatwg-archive, public-html, ietf-http-wg and public-webapps.

## 5.2 Experiment Setup

**Threshold Setting.** According to the definition of important emails, we should set a threshold to identify important emails. Generally, the threshold can be set based on the data analysis. We analyse the distribution of email importance scores in our dataset as shown in Fig. 4. We set the threshold to be 2 in our experiment, which represents that the top 7% of the highest-scoring emails are considered to be important emails.

**Evalution Metric.** We choose the AUC curve as the evaluation method since it is more insensitive to unbalanced data. An email with higher AUC score means that it's more likely to get higher importance score.

**Baselines.** We have selected three methods as baselines, including TrustMail [6], Importance Ranking (IR) [1] and Content Ranking (CR) [20]. Inspired by Trust-Mail, we use the trust score of senders to predict emails' importance. Firstly we build a social network based on the number of emails between each user. Then we use PageRank [12] to obtain the trust score of each user. Finally, we find the

---

[5] http://scikit-learn.org.
[6] For email importance prediction with XGBoost, we set learning_rate = 0.1, n_estimators = 1000, max_depth = 5, min_child_weight = 1, gamma = 0, subsample = 0.8, colsample_bytree = 0.8, objective = 'binary:logistic', scale_pos_weight = 1, seed = 27.

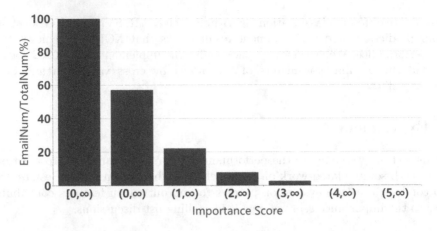

**Fig. 4.** Email importance distribution of our dataset.

threshold for sender trust score of important emails based on training the annotated data. In addition, we adapt the Importance Ranking (IR) algorithm used for Gmail Priority Inbox. Since the detailed features are not described and there is no label features in mailing lists, we use social, content and thread features in our implementation. Content Ranking (CR) is the method which only considers the content features of emails. In this approach we extract N-gram features, part-of-speech tags, length features and content features for email classification.

### 5.3 Experiment Result and Analyse

**Prediction Model Results.** Figure 5 shows ROC curves for all methods of important email prediction. We can see that our learning method outperforms baselines with large gains, which proved that the features we propose are effective for the prediction of important emails. Our learning method outperforms other methods as expect since TrustMail only considers the social interactions between users and the other two baselines focus on part of the features we propose.

**Feature Importance Evaluation.** First, we analyse the relative importance of different feature groups. Table 2 shows the AUC scores when we use only one feature group, and the groups are ordered by AUC scores. The results suggest that temporal feature is less important. Considering the fact that emails may be subject to manual moderation in mailing lists, recipients can't feedback timely. This fact has a huge negative effect on temporal features. Thread and social features do contribute to the importance of emails in mailing list discussions. Content features show the best performance which is consistent with the conclusion of [20].

Then we analyse the relative importance of each individual feature. We use the same method for individual feature evaluation and the effective individual

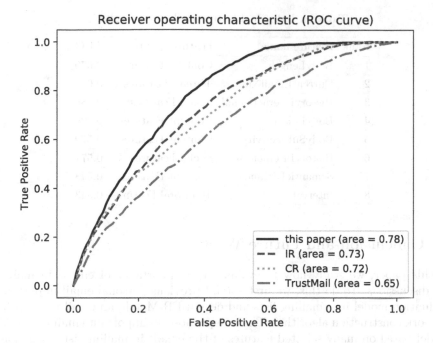

**Fig. 5.** Prediction model results.

**Table 2.** Feature group evaluation results.

| Feature | AUC | | | | | |
|---|---|---|---|---|---|---|
| | Dataset | | | | | |
| | www-style | whatwg | public-html | ietf-http-wg | webapps | All |
| Content features | 0.714 | 0.705 | 0.719 | 0.698 | 0.728 | 0.730 |
| Thread features | 0.599 | 0.689 | 0.630 | 0.628 | 0.618 | 0.628 |
| Social features | 0.589 | 0.600 | 0.606 | 0.608 | 0.617 | 0.605 |
| Temporal features | 0.579 | 0.597 | 0.512 | 0.548 | 0.548 | 0.555 |
| All features | 0.784 | 0.760 | 0.735 | 0.764 | 0.782 | 0.787 |

features are illustrated in Table 3. In general, the results are consistent with previous feature group evaluation results. 'EmailLength' and 'CurrentEmailNum' features obviously have better performance than other features, which conforms to our common sense. We are likely to regard an email as important if it has rich contents. And it is also indicated that Matthew effect [11] exists in mailing list discussions. The more emails involved in discussions, the more likely people will participate in the discussions and new emails are more likely to have more responses. The semantic distance of each email does contribute to email importance. In addition, we find that some features such as 'SubjectLength', 'TimeOfDay', 'TimeOfWeek' contribute little to email importance.

**Table 3.** Individual feature evaluation results.

| Rank | Feature name | Feature group | AUC |
|------|--------------|---------------|-----|
| 1 | BodyLength | Content Features | 0.679 |
| 2 | CurrentEmailNum | Thread Features | 0.621 |
| 3 | HistoryInteractEmail | Social Features | 0.586 |
| 4 | BodyPolarity | Content Features | 0.580 |
| 5 | BodySubjectivity | Content Features | 0.579 |
| 6 | HistoryInteractUser | Social Features | 0.571 |
| 7 | SemanticDistance | Content Features | 0.548 |
| 8 | Interval | Temporal Features | 0.543 |

## 6    Conclusion and Future Work

In this paper, we study how to evaluate the importance of emails in mailing list discussions. To do this, we first extend previous personal email importance evaluation model into mailing lists and design ER-Match, an email relationship network construction algorithm. Then we propose an important email prediction model based on many selected features of the emails in mailing list discussions. We study which features might contribute more to the importance of emails in mailing list discussions. Experiment with publicly available mailing lists shows that our prediction model outperforms all baselines. What's more, we find that among all the features, content features are more likely to influence the importance of emails. Our findings provide new insights about how people participate in mailing list discussions. In addition, the email thread structure that we design takes direct and indirect quotation relationship into consideration, which could also contributes to email search, email summary and email visualization. In future work, the email importance prediction model in this paper will be extended with more features, and we will try to obtain manual annotated data to improve the effectiveness of the prediction model.

**Acknowledgement.** This work is supported by National Key Research & Development Program (2016YFB1000503).

## References

1. Aberdeen, D., Pacovsky, O., Slater, A.: The learning behind gmail priority inbox. In: LCCC: NIPS 2010 Workshop on Learning on Cores, Clusters and Clouds (2010)
2. Albitar, S., Fournier, S., Espinasse, B.: An effective TF/IDF-based text-to-text semantic similarity measure for text classification. In: Benatallah, B., Bestavros, A., Manolopoulos, Y., Vakali, A., Zhang, Y. (eds.) WISE 2014. LNCS, vol. 8786, pp. 105–114. Springer, Cham (2014). https://doi.org/10.1007/978-3-319-11749-2_8
3. Chen, T., Guestrin, C.: XGBoost: a scalable tree boosting system. In: Proceedings of the 22nd ACM SIGKDD International Conference on Knowledge Discovery and Data Mining, pp. 785–794. ACM (2016)

 4. Dabbish, L.A., Kraut, R.E., Fussell, S., Kiesler, S.: Understanding email use: predicting action on a message. In: Proceedings of the SIGCHI Conference on Human Factors in Computing Systems, pp. 691–700. ACM (2005)
 5. Dehghani, M., Shakery, A., Asadpour, M., Koushkestani, A.: A learning approach for email conversation thread reconstruction. J. Inf. Sci. **39**(6), 846–863 (2013)
 6. Golbeck, J., Hendler, J.: Inferring binary trust relationships in web-based social networks. ACM Tran. Internet Technol. (TOIT) **6**(4), 497–529 (2006)
 7. Jain, A.: XGboost tuning. https://www.analyticsvidhya.com/blog/2016/03/complete-guide-parameter-tuning-xgboost-with-codes-python/. Accessed 24 July 2018
 8. Joshi, S., Contractor, D., Ng, K., Deshpande, P.M., Hampp, T.: Auto-grouping emails for faster e-discovery. Proc. VLDB Endow. **4**(12), 1284–1294 (2011)
 9. Lewis, D.D., Knowles, K.A.: Threading electronic mail: a preliminary study. Inf. Process. Manage. **33**(2), 209–217 (1997)
10. Liu, L., Tang, J., Han, J., Jiang, M., Yang, S.: Mining topic-level influence in heterogeneous networks. In: CIKM ACM Conference on Information and Knowledge Management, CIKM 2010, Toronto, Ontario, Canada, October, pp. 199–208 (2010)
11. Merton, R.K.: The Matthew effect in science: the reward and communication systems of science are considered. Science **159**(3810), 56–63 (1968)
12. Page, L.: The pagerank citation ranking: bringing order to the web. Stanford Digital Libraries Working Paper **9**(1), 1–14 (1999)
13. Passant, A., Zimmermann, A., Schneider, J., Breslin, J.G.: A semantic framework for modelling quotes in email conversations. In: Proceedings of the 1st International Conference on Intelligent Semantic Web-Services and Applications. ACM (2010)
14. Sharaff, A., Nagwani, N.K.: Email thread identification using latent Dirichlet allocation and non-negative matrix factorization based clustering techniques. J. Inf. Sci. **42**(2), 200–212 (2016)
15. Tsugawa, S., Ohsaki, H., Imase, M.: Estimating message importance using inferred inter-recipient trust for supporting email triage. Inf. Media Technol. **7**(3), 1073–1082 (2012)
16. Wu, Y., Oard, D.W.: Indexing emails and email threads for retrieval. In: Proceedings of the 28th Annual International ACM SIGIR Conference on Research and Development in Information Retrieval, pp. 665–666. ACM (2005)
17. Yang, L., Dumais, S.T., Bennett, P.N., Awadallah, A.H.: Characterizing and predicting enterprise email reply behavior. In: Proceedings of the 40th International ACM SIGIR Conference on Research and Development in Information Retrieval, pp. 235–244. ACM (2017)
18. Yoo, S., Yang, Y., Lin, F., Moon, I.C.: Mining social networks for personalized email prioritization. In: Proceedings of the 15th ACM SIGKDD International Conference on Knowledge Discovery and Data Mining, pp. 967–976. ACM (2009)
19. Zawinski, J.: Message threading. https://www.jwz.org/doc/threading.html/. Accessed 10 May 2018
20. Zhang, F., Xu, K.: Annotation and classification of an email importance corpus. In: Proceedings of the 53rd Annual Meeting of the Association for Computational Linguistics and the 7th International Joint Conference on Natural Language Processing (Volume 2: Short Papers), vol. 2, pp. 651–656 (2015)

# SETTRUST: Social Exchange Theory Based Context-Aware Trust Prediction in Online Social Networks

Seyed Mohssen Ghafari$^{(\boxtimes)}$, Shahpar Yakhchi, Amin Beheshti, and Mehmet Orgun

Macquarie University, Sydney, Australia
{seyed-mohssen.ghafari,Shahpar.Yakhchi}@hdr.mq.edu.au,
seyedmohssen.ghafari@data61.csiro.au,
{amin.beheshti,mehmet.orgun}@mq.edu.au

**Abstract.** Trust is context-dependent. In real-world scenarios, people trust each other only in certain contexts. However, this concept has not been seriously taken into account in most of the existing trust prediction approaches in Online Social Networks (OSNs). In addition, very few attempts have been made on trust prediction based on social psychology theories. For decades, social psychology theories have attempted to explain people's behaviors in social networks; hence, employing such theories for trust prediction in OSNs will enhance accuracy. In this paper, we apply a well-known psychology theory, called Social Exchange Theory (SET), to evaluate the potential trust relation between users in OSNs. Based on SET, one person starts a relationship with another person, if and only if the costs of that relationship are less than its benefits. To evaluate potential trust relations in OSNs based on SET, we first propose some factors to capture the costs and benefits of a relationship. Then, based on these factors, we propose a trust metric called *Trust Degree*; at that point, we propose a trust prediction method, based on Matrix Factorization and apply the context of trust in a mathematical model. Finally, we conduct experiments on two real-world datasets to demonstrate the superior performance of our approach over the state-of-the-art approaches.

**Keywords:** Trust prediction · Social networks analytics · Social Exchange Theory · Fake news

## 1 Introduction

Online Social Networks (OSNs) have become the most popular interaction platforms, attracting a vast volume of users. OSNs are able to link people who have similar interests and mindsets regardless of their locations, culture, religious beliefs, and so on. OSNs have played an important role in people's daily life. For example, a study of Althoff et al. [34] indicates that surprisingly OSNs

© Springer Nature Switzerland AG 2019
H. Hacid et al. (Eds.): QUAT 2018, LNCS 11235, pp. 46–61, 2019.
https://doi.org/10.1007/978-3-030-19143-6_4

have a great impact on both online and offline behaviors of their users. More-over, OSNs have become more and more popular in recent years. According to Lenhart et al. [1], a large number of teens and young people stopped blogging since 2006, and started to become the users of OSNs [1]. They also reported that in 2010, 73% of American teens used OSNs. In addition, in 2010, 52% of adults had two or more accounts on different OSNs [1]. While OSNs are playing substantial roles in people's lives, many challenges have emerged, one of which is the issue of trust relation between the users in OSNs.

**Trust**, as Mayer et al. [28] have defined, is "the willingness of a party to be vulnerable to the actions of another party based on the expectation that the other will perform a particular action important to the trustor, irrespective of the ability to monitor or control that other party" [28]. Trust is one of the main factors that influence one user to start a relation with another user, believe in what the other user shares, recommends and provides advice about, and so on. Moreover, trust is context-dependent. This means that if person A trusts person B, this trust value is achieved in a certain context of trust. For instance, assume that A is a PhD student in computer science and B is his supervisor and a professor. A trusts B in the context of computer science. But does A trust B in photography or football? The answer is likely to be "no".

**Trust Prediction** aims to predict the potential trust relation between two users in OSNs who in many cases have not interacted before [38]. In the lit-erature, there are two types of trust prediction approaches. In the first type, Sanadhya and Singh [32] proposed an approach, called Trust-ACO, which is based on the Ant Colony algorithm to predict trust relations. Wang et al. [39] investigated the impact of Social Status theory on trust prediction in OSNs. Jang et al. [25] proposed a new trust prediction approach based on Belief Propagation algorithm. In addition, Beigi et al. [12] proposed an emotional trust/distrust pre-diction approach called ETD to consider the emotional information in the trust prediction procedure. Furthermore, Tang et al. [24] proposed a new trust pre-diction model, named hTrust based on Homophily Theory. However, these trust prediction approaches did not consider the context of trust and assumed that all the trust relations are the same.

In the second type, in the literature, there are a few studies on context-aware trust predictions. Liu et al. [19] proposed a contextual social network structure to deal with several social contextual factors [2]. Moreover, Zheng et al. [38] proposed the first context-aware trust prediction mechanism. They considered the personal properties and interpersonal properties of users for trust prediction. Another approach that considered the context of trust was proposed by Wang et al. [40]. They proposed the first context-aware trust inference model for OSNs. Their model can infer the trust values between the users that are connecting together, otherwise it cannot predict the trust value between the users.

**Research Gaps.** The trust prediction approaches in the literature have some drawbacks as follows: (i) The research community has mainly focused on predict-ing trust relations between users regardless the context of these trust relations.

(ii) There are only a few context-aware trust prediction approaches in the literature. We divide their drawbacks into two subgroups (a) They require previous interactions of the users. As it was indicated in [24], "online trust relations follow a power law distribution, suggesting that a small number of users specify many trust relations while a large proportion of users specify a few trust relations" [24], then, context-aware trust prediction approaches, like [19] and [40] suffer from the unavailability of enough trust relations and this could have a negative impact on the accuracy of these approaches [39] (that is, they suffer from the Data Sparsity Problem). (b) They require lots of information about the user. Because of the information that the context-aware approaches, like [38] require for their trust prediction procedures, they cannot be applied in many cases in OSNs. These approaches need to know the locations, the preferences, social intimacy and other information of the users, which is usually not available in many real-world cases in OSNs. As a result, the existing context-aware trust prediction approaches either cannot deal with the data sparsity problem, or only focused on some ideal occasions that they can have access to many users' information.

**Our Approach and Contributions.** We employ a well-known social psychology theory, SET [17,22,37], to predict the potential trust relations between the users in OSNs. At that point, based on some social context factors and Matrix Factorization (MF), we propose a novel trust prediction approach. The unique contributions of this paper are:

- To the best of our knowledge, this is the first approach that employs the Social Exchange Theory for a context-aware trust prediction in OSNs.
- We propose a factor, called Bad Language Detection, which can detect the swear words in users' social information items such as tweets on Twitters, posts on Facebook and/or reviews on Amazon.
- We propose a trust prediction model based on Social Exchange Theory and Matrix Factorization (MF) which, in contrast to many of the existing approaches, is one of the few approaches that consider the context of trust.
- We evaluate our proposed models on two real-world datasets and the results demonstrate the superior performance of our models compared to the state-of-the-art trust prediction approaches.

The rest of the paper is organized as follows: Sect. 2 presents related works and Sect. 3 also presents a description of SET and its application in OSNs. The proposed trust prediction model are discussed in Sect. 4. The experimental evaluation presented in Sect. 5. Sections 5.4 and 6 present the discussion and conclusion sections, respectively.

## 2   Related Work

In this section, we review the existing studies in two groups: trust prediction approaches without considering the context of trust, and context-aware trust prediction approaches.

## 2.1    Contextual Trust Prediction

The notion of trust is context-dependent. Therefore, trusting someone under one type of context does not guarantee trusting her in other types [36]. Moreover, **context** (which influences in the building of a trust relationship between the trustor and the trustee [26]) is multi-faceted [38]. In social society, the context about the interaction between two participants can be considered as the *Social Context* and the *Interaction Context* can provide more information such as the type or time of services, location and so on [38]. In addition, context-aware approaches try to consider different social context factors to evaluate a potential trust relation.

## 2.2    Context-Less Approaches

The context-less approaches do not distinguish between different types of trust relations in OSNs. They can be roughly divided into two groups: unsupervised [30] and supervised [21] methods. Supervised methods treat the trust prediction problem as a classification problem, where trustable users have been labeled after extracting some features from available sources [4,5,15]. Unsupervised approaches make a trust prediction with the help of some trust network properties, such as trust propagation [20]. The performance of trust prediction in the most of existing methods can be affected by the lack of available data (data sparsity problem). The approach presented in hTrust [24], indicates performance improvement of trust prediction based on one of the well-known social theories, Homophily [24], to show that two similar users have a higher potential to establish a trust relationship. In addition, in sTrust [39], another social psychology based trust prediction approach, which is based on social status theory, users with higher statuses can have a higher chance to be considered as trustworthy users. We observe that, all of the above approaches neglect to consider the context of trust, which can have a significant impact on the performance of trust prediction.

## 2.3    Context-Aware Approaches

Liu et al. [19] highlighted the importance of the context of trust as an essential factor for trust prediction approaches. However, minor efforts have been conducted in the literature to consider the context of trust. In this line of work, Zheng et al. [38] proposed a context-aware approach to take both the user's properties and features of contexts into account. Social trust proposed as a novel probabilistic social context-aware trust inference approach, exploits some textual information to deliver better results [40]. In this approach, trust is inferred along the paths connecting two users. Thus, if two users are not connected by any path, no trust between them can be predicted. Similar to this approach, Liu et al. [18] proposed a context-aware trust prediction approach based on the web-of-trust concept and considered some social context factors, such as users'

location, previous interactions, social intimacy degree with other users, the existing trust relations and so on. Although these studies put the first step towards
considering the context of trust as a key factor, their success is not guaranteed
because of their high dependency to the concept of web-of-trust and due to the
data sparsity problem.

*Added Value of Our Approach.* There are very few studies reported in the literature that try to focus on the context of trust. There are two drawbacks as follows.
One is that some of these approaches require lots of information about the users,
in order to make proper and accurate predictions. Another is that there are no
particular mechanisms in the context-aware trust prediction approaches to deal
with the data sparsity problem, particulary in the cases in which they require
the previous interactions of users for trust prediction.

## 3   Social Exchange Theory and Its Applications in OSNs

Social Exchange theory [17,22,37] is one of the basic social psychology theories
that explains the nature of social interactions with the help of a Costs-Benefits
structure. Based on this theory, People prefer to participate in a relationship
that has low costs and brings them the maximum benefits [17,22,37].

$$SET = Benefit - Cost > 0 \tag{1}$$

Hence, if the SET of a relationship is negative for one or all the participants,
that relationship will probably break down in the future. It is worth to mention
that there are some other factors that may have an impact on breaking down or
establishing a relationship, like the level of alternatives or level of expectations.
However, we do not consider them in this paper and leave them for our future
work. The factors, like time and money that someone spent or will spend in his or
her relationship, the information that he or she should share in this relationship,
the negative points that the other party of this relation has, and so on, represent
the costs of a relationship. Moreover, the services that he or she receives, the
knowledge or money that he or she acquires, the possible happiness that he or she
may obtain, are part of the benefits of this relationship. It should be considered
that these relations include all the possible relationships that people could have
with each other, like the relations between student-supervisor, football player-
coach, doctor-patient, user-broadband service provider, and so on.

There have been some studies on the effects of SET on OSNs. For instance,
Surma et al. [33] investigate the existence of SET on Facebook. They note that
any relationship requires a starting point and one of the participants should
make the first move [33]. This may include any answer from another partici-
pant indicating the behavioral exchange. In [33], they consider the Likes that
a user received from his or her friends during the past week on his or her posts.
They study the fact that how many of the users Liked back the posts of other
participants. Moreover, they also consider some other factors like gender, age,
posts sent, and comments received. Their experimental results demonstrate the

existence of Social Exchange Theory in OSNs. Another study was conducted by Barak [33] on influential factors that partners may have on online dating websites. Their approach is based on SET and it focus on users' features, like marital status, the level of education, income, and their appearance [33]. The outcomes of their research illustrate that users look for people with the same marital status or better features like income and education [33].

**Motivating Example.** Alice is a postgraduate student in computer science, and David and Samuel are university professors. Alice wants to continue her studies at the PhD level and she needs to find a supervisor for her PhD studies. Alice would compare the benefits and costs of supervision of David and Samuel. Alice is interested to work in Social Media Analysis. Based on SET, at first, Alice lists all the possible pros and cons of being a student of both the supervisors. Assume that on one hand, David's expertise is in Cloud Computing, he is a kind man, he has lots of great publications (Benefits), and he has not supervised any PhD students before (Costs). On the other hand, Samuel works on Social Media Analysis, he has supervised many PhD students before, and he also has great publications (Benefits). However, he is a harsh man at the workplace (Cost). in Alice's mind, the negative point of Samuel (being a harsh man at the workplace) is much less than its positive points. In addition, the negative point of Samuel's supervision is less than the negative points of the supervision of David (having a different area of interest and having no experience of supervising PhD students). Hence, Alice decides to choose Samuel (Fig. 1).

**Fig. 1.** The proposed TDTrust framework

# 4   SETTrust: A Context-Aware Trust Prediction Approach

In this section, we will describe our proposed trust prediction methodology.

## 4.1   Social Context Factors

In this section, we describe the social context factors that we employ in our trust prediction approach.

A. *Level of Expertise.* "A recommendation from an expert person in a certain domain is more acceptable compared to the less knowledgeable person" [40]. In this paper, we define the Level of Expertise of a target user like our previous work [31]: (i) the activeness of a user in a specific context: if he/she wrote posts/reviews equal or more than the average number of posts/reviews of other users'; and (ii) other users' opinion regarding these posts/reviews. For instance, consider that Jack (a user in OSNs) has written many reviews/posts related to politic and they were highly rated by other. In contrast, Mary just has wrote two reviews/posts on politics and they have not received any ratings. Hence, in the topic of politics, Jack could be more trustworthy in the other users' mind.

Let $U = ...u_m$ denote the set of users, and $C = ...c_k$ the set of contexts of trust relations. Let $n_i$ denotes the posts/reviews numbers for user $u_i$, i = 1, ..., m, and $n_{i,c_k}$ the total number of post/reviews by user $u_i$ in context $c_k$ for i = 1, ..., m and j = 1, ..., k. Let $a_{i,c_k}$ denote the status of user $u_i$ where $a_{i,c_k} = 0$ means $u_i$ is inactive and $a_{i,c_k} = 1$ means $u_i$ is active. Each review/post can receive a score from other users $s$ (it can be in scale of 1 to 3, on Likert scale, i.e., a psychometric scale commonly involved in research that employs questionnaires).

$$a_{i,c_k} = \begin{cases} 1, & \text{if } n_{i,c_k} >= \dfrac{\sum_{r=1}^{m} n_{r,c_k}}{m} \\ 0, & \text{otherwise} \end{cases} \tag{2}$$

the average score that other users gave to posts/reviews of $u_i$ in $c_k$ can be evaluated by:

$$S_{i,c_k} = \frac{1}{n_{i,c_k}} \sum_{r=1}^{n_{i,c_k}} s_r^{i,c_k}, \tag{3}$$

where $s_r^{i,c_k}$ is the score value of $r_{th}$ review of $u_i$ that was archived in $c_k$. At the end, the level of expertise $u_i$ in the $c_k$ can be calculated by:

$$v_{i,c_k} = S_{i,c_k} \times n_{i,c_k} \tag{4}$$

B. *Interest.* "Interest could be conceived of as an individual's attitude towards a set of objects" [40]. In this research, we consider $p_{ic_k}$ as the interest of $u_i$ in the context $c_k$, which means the topics/categories of items that a user's posts/reviews belong to. It is within the scope of $c_k$ when $p_{ic_k} = 1$, and it is not when $p_{ic_k} = 0$. Furthermore, if both the source user $u_i$ and the target user $u_j$ have the same interest in the same context $c_k$, $P_{ijc_k} = 1$, and otherwise $P_{ijc_k} = -1$.

**C. *Number of Followers.*** In this paper, $NoF_A$ denotes the number of followers of user $A$, and is equal to the "number of followers"/"number of people who read and rated the user's reviews". Assume that David has a higher number of follower compared to Sarah. It has been validated in Social Science theories [18], that the recommendation from David (with a larger number of followers) is more credible.

**D. *Bad Language Detection.*** Machiavellian, Psychopathic traits were significantly positively correlated with swear words [14]. A user who use swearing words and bad language in OSNs, can lose his intimacy with the other users. The Dark Triad (i.e. Machiavellianism, Psychopathy and Narcissism) seem to reflect traits that would render someone a candidate for avoidance. Given the traits associated with Psychopathy it would often be advantageous for others to acquiesce to or avoid such individuals [16]. Hence in this research, based on the LIWC and text mining analysis, we aim to detect the bad language usage in posts/reviews and consider it as a negative point in trustworthiness of the user. We can evaluate the level of Bad language $u_i$ in the context $c_k$ follows:

$$Bl_{ic_k} = \frac{B_{i,c_k}}{W_{i,c_k}} \tag{5}$$

where $B_{i,c_k}$ is the total number of swearing words, which have been written by $u_i$ in the context $c_k$, in this formula, $W_{i,c_k}$ represents the total number of words that he wrote in his posts/reviews in the context $c_k$.

## 4.2   Trust Prediction Mechanism

We present algorithms, for predicting trust values in OSNs, employing social context factors inspired by Social Exchange Theory. For trust prediction, we propose the following formula:

$$SET_{ijc_k} = w_1(P_{ijc_k}) + w_2 \times v_{jc_k} + w_3 \times NoF_j - w_4 \times Bl_{jc_k}, \tag{6}$$

where $SET_{ijc_k}$ is the trust degree that we employ to predict the trust value between $u_i$ and $u_j$ in the context $c_k$, and $w_z$, $z = \{1, \cdots, 4\}$, is the controlling parameter to control the impact of social contextual parameters. In the above formula, calculate the Cost and Benefit of the relation between $u_i$ and $u_j$. For instance, in one hand, $Bl_{jc_k}$, having different interests ($P_{ijc_k} = -1$), having a low level of expertise of $u_j$, and having a low number of followers for $u_j$ can be considered as the Cost of that relationship. In the other hand, lack of $Bl_{jc_k}$, having the same interests ($P_{ijc_k} = 1$), having a high level of expertise of $u_j$, and having a high number of followers for $u_j$ are the singes of Benefit of that relationship. Since $NoF_j$ could be a large number, we normalize it to the rage of 0 and 1 by feature scaling as:

$$NoF_j' = \frac{NoF_j - min(NoF)}{max(NoF) - min(NoF)} \qquad (7)$$

**Problem Statement.** Suppose we have $n$ users $U = \{u_1, \cdots, u_n\}$, and $G \in R^{n \times n}$ be a square matrix that contains the trust relations between users, where $G(i, j) = 1$ means $u_i$ trusts $u_j$, and $G(i, j) = 0$ indicates there is no trust relation between $u_i$ and $u_j$. The $G$ matrix is sparse in OSNs [24], and thus in order to deal with this data sparsity, the $U$ low-ranked matrix as $U \in R^{n \times d}$, $d << n$ should be extracted. Tang et al. [24] propose a trust prediction approach based on Matrix Factorization (MF) as follows:

$$min_{U,H}\|G - UHU^T\|_F^2 + \alpha \times (\|U\|_F^2 + \|H\|_F^2), U > 0, H > 0, \qquad (8)$$

where $U$ represents the users' interest, $d$ represents the facets of these interests, and $H$ matrix contains compact correlations among $U$ [39]. Hence, based on the studies of Wang et al. [39] and Tang et al. [24] we propose:

$$\begin{aligned} SET_{ijc_k} \times (UHU^T) &= 0 \\ SET_{ijc_k} \times (UHU^T) &= 1 \end{aligned} \qquad (9)$$

We propose the following term, and the aim of SET regularisation is to maximizing this term:

$$\sum_i^n \sum_{j!=i}^n (max\{0, f(SET_{ijc_k})(UHU^T)\}^2) \qquad (10)$$

At that point, we propose a trust prediction model based on matrix factorization as follows:

$$min_{U,H}\|G - UHU^T\|_F^2 + \lambda \times (\sum_i^n \sum_{j!=i}^n (max\{0, f(SET_{ijc_k})(UHU^T)\}^2)) \\ + \alpha \times \|U\|_F^2 + \alpha \times \|H\|_F^2), U > 0, H > 0, \qquad (11)$$

where $\lambda$ is a controlling parameter. In this paper, we assume that we have $k$ context of trust as $C = \{c_1, c_2, \cdots, c_k\}$.

**Modeling Proposed Trust Prediction.** Next, if we assume $B = SET_{ijc_k}$, we propose an updating schema for both U and H based on [13]:

$$U(i, j) \leftarrow U(i, j)\sqrt{\frac{D(i, j)}{E(i, j)}} \qquad (12)$$

$$H(i,j) \leftarrow H(i,j)\sqrt{\frac{P(i,j)}{Y(i,j)}}, \tag{13}$$

where:

$$D = 2GUH^T + 2G^TUH \tag{14}$$

$$\begin{aligned} E = 2H^TUU^THU + 2HUU^THU + \lambda \times UU^THU \odot B \odot B^T \\ + \lambda \times H^TU \odot B \odot B^T \odot UTH^TU \\ + \lambda \times HU \odot B \odot B^T \odot UTHU + \lambda \\ \times H^TUU^TH^TU \odot B \odot B^T + 2\alpha U \end{aligned} \tag{15}$$

$$P = 2U^TGHU + 2G^TUHU^T \tag{16}$$

$$\begin{aligned} Y = U^TU^ThU^TU + UUHU^TU + \lambda \times (B \odot UHU^T \odot B \odot U \\ + U \odot B^T \odot U^THU \odot B^T \odot U^T) + 2\alpha H \end{aligned} \tag{17}$$

---

**Algorithm 1.** Trust Prediction with SETTrust

---

1: Establishing the SET in each context
2: Randomly initializing $U, H, C$
3: **while** It is not the convergent state **do**
4:     Initializing D, E, P, Y, based on the formulas (14-17)
5:     for i = 1 to m do
6:         for j = 1 to r do

7:         $U(i,j) \leftarrow U(i,j)\sqrt{\dfrac{D(i,j)}{E(i,j)}}$

8:         $H(i,j) \leftarrow H(i,j)\sqrt{\dfrac{P(i,j)}{Y(i,j)}}$

9:         end for
10:     end for
11: **end while**
12: return $U, H$

---

**Summary.** We presented a context-aware trust prediction approach based on SET. We want to know how this approach can help to predict the trust relations between users. Firstly, it considers the context of trust. Hence, it considers some social context factors that can represent the context of a potential trust relation. When we a have a pair of users (a source user and a target user), SETTrust checks whether the target user is expert in a specific context, are they both have the same preference in that particular context, how many people follow the target user, and what sort of behavior the target user has (from the point of view of using swear words) in OSNs. Finally, based on the trust degree that SETTrust establishes between these users and with the help of MF (Algorithm 1), SETTrust will predict the trust value between them. It is worth mentioning that, SETTrust does not need to know much information about the users; in contrast to current context-aware approaches, it also does not need the current trust relations between users to infer other trust relations or it does not need to have any information about previous interactions of source or target user, which can make it a feasible solution to deal with the data sparsity problem.

## 5    Experiments

### 5.1    Experimental Setup

To evaluate our approach and compared it with four baseline approaches, we employ two real-world datasets, named Epinions and Ciao [36]. These datasets contain the reviews, the ratings, the trust relations between of users, and we only considered users who had more than 3 reviews. We compare our approach with four other approaches: (i) hTrust [24]: it is based on the Homophily Theory and it was reviewed in Sect. 2. (ii) sTrust [39]: it is based on the Social Status theory and it was reviewed in Sect. 2. (iii) Zheng [38]: it also was reviewed in Sect. 2. (iv) Random Trust Prediction: it randomly assigns a trust value to users.

We divide each of these datasets into two parts. The first one is the users who do not have any trust relations (N) and the other one that includes the users who have trust relations with other users (T). We sort these trust relations based on the time of establishment of their relations. At that point, we select $A\%$ of them as the Old trust relations and $(1 - A)\%$ of them as the New trust relations. We consider 4% values for $A = \{60, 70, 80, 90\}$. Furthermore, we employ a trust prediction metric from [29] to evaluate the performance of our approach. Based on this approach, we first merge the New trust relations and the non-trust relations ($N \cap New$) and call them M. Then, with the help of SETTRUST and other trust prediction approaches in this experiment, we want to predict the trust relations in M, and extract |N| number of trust relations and call it Predict. Based on this method, the performance of any trust prediction approach could be determined by the following formula:

$$\frac{|New \cap Predict|}{|New|} \tag{18}$$

It is worth to mention that, SETTRUST can reach its highest performance with $\lambda = 0.5$ and $\alpha = 0.1$. We investigate the effects of the different $\lambda$ values on SETTRUST in the subsection 5.6. Moreover, we did not consider the Bad Language Detection factor in our experiments and leave it for our future works.

**Table 1.** Datasets statistics

|                              | Ciao   | Epinions |
|------------------------------|--------|----------|
| Numb. of users               | 1000   | 1050     |
| Min. numb. of reviews per users | 3   | 3        |
| Trust network density        | 0.0087 | 0.0093   |
| Numb. trust relations        | 8726   | 10264    |

## 5.2  Experimental Results

The experimental results on Ciao and Epinions datasets are illustrated in Tables 1 and 2, respectively. It can be observed that SETTrust outperformed other approaches in both datasets. For example, when the size of A is 90%, SETTrust is more than 33%, about 47%, 4.28 times, and 600 times more accurate compared to Zheng, hTrust, sTrust, and Random, respectively. After SETTrust, Zheng has the best performance. For instance, when the size of A is equal to 90%, Zheng is 20%, 2.84 times, and 398 times more accurate than hTrust, sTrust, and Random, respectively. Next, hTrust has the best performance compared to the sTrust and Random, and Random has the lowest trust prediction accuracy among all five approaches (Table 3).

**Table 2.** Experimental results on Ciao dataset

| Approach | 60% | 70% | 80% | 90% |
|----------|-----|-----|-----|-----|
| SETTrust | 0.31 | 0.36 | 0.42 | 0.6 |
| Zheng | 0.29 | 0.3 | 0.367 | 0.398 |
| hTrust | 0.259 | 0.28 | 0.319 | 0.32 |
| sTrust | 0.06 | 0.1 | 0.13 | 0.14 |
| Random | 0.0008 | 0.00089 | 0.00097 | 0.001 |

**Table 3.** Experimental results on Epinions dataset

| Approach | 60% | 70% | 80% | 90% |
|----------|-----|-----|-----|-----|
| SETTrust | 0.49 | 0.51 | 0.53 | 0.55 |
| Zheng | 0.341 | 0.386 | 0.402 | 0.426 |
| hTrust | 0.29 | 0.288 | 0.289 | 0.297 |
| sTrust | 0.0043 | 0.0044 | 0.00456 | 0.005 |
| Random | 0.0001 | 0.00015 | 0.00019 | 0.00023 |

## 5.3  The TDTrust Regularization Effects

In this paper, $\lambda$ is a controlling parameter for SETTrust effects. Here we want to investigate the effects of $\lambda$ on SETTrust's accuracy. Hence, we considered $\lambda = \{0.1, 0.5, 0.8, 0.9, 10\}$. The result illustrate that: (i) the highest accuracy of SETTrust is when $\lambda = 0.5$; (ii) whenever $\lambda$ increases from 0 to 0.5, we see an increase in the accuracy of SETTrust; and (iii) when $\lambda > 0.5$, the accuracy of SETTrust decreases, especially for $\lambda > 1$. Figure 2 can illustrates the different level of accuracy for SETTrust.

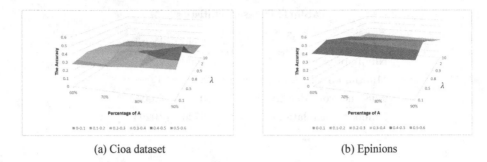

(a) Cioa dataset                              (b) Epinions

**Fig. 2.** Effects of SETTrust regularization

## 5.4  Discussion

The experimental results demonstrate that SETTRUST has the best performance compared to four other approaches in all values of A (60, 70, 80, 90).
The first reason for sTrust to have a such performance is that it is a context-less
approach. However, why the accuracy of sTrust is lower than hTrust? It may
be because of the fact that the only factor that sTrust considers is the status of
users. This factor may not be enough to capture the trust value between users.
There are many users in both Epinions and Ciao datasets which have a high
status, but most of the users do not trust them.

Although hTrust is also a context-less method, since it employs some other
trust evaluation metrics, like rating similarity and rating style similarity, it is
more accurate than sTrust. Furthermore, one of the reasons that Zheng has a
lower accuracy compared to SETTrust is that it relies on some social context
factors like intimacy degree, which represents the frequency of previous interactions between the users and it may not be available in most of the real-world
scenarios (because of the data sparsity problem).

Moreover, the low performance of Random may be because of its randomly
trust allocation procedure. Finally, the main reason for having a high accuracy
for SETTrust is the fact that it considers the context of trust. So in SETTrust
if a user is trustworthy in one context, he/she may be untrustworthy in another
context. Considering this difference can have a huge improvement on the trust
prediction accuracy of any approach. In addition, SETTrust only relies on the
social context factors that may be available in any OSNs and do not need some
extra information about the users, like their location, previous interactions, intimacy degree, etc. However, since the trust values in an OSN are not fixed values
and it could be changed over the time, SETTrust may fail to provide a dynamic
trust value for each pair of users. For instance, a user may be trustworthy for
a while and become untrustworthy (shares deceptive information, shares fake
news, etc.) after awhile. In our future work, one of the dimensions that could
improve the SETTrust is the fact that it should also consider the time-based
relationships [3,27]. Finally, for checking the content of the news we focus on
Information extraction [8–10].

# 6 Conclusion and Future Works

Trust prediction is one of the main challenges in OSNs. We have proposed a new context-aware trust prediction approach for OSNs, called SETTRUST. To the best of our knowledge, this is the first approach that employs the Social Exchange Theory for a context-aware trust prediction in OSNs. We proposed a factor, called Bad Language Detection, which can detect the swear words in users' social information items such as tweets on Twitters, posts on Facebook and/or reviews on Amazon. We proposed a trust prediction model based on Social Exchange Theory and Matrix Factorization (MF) which, in contrast to many of the existing approaches, is one of the few approaches that consider the context of trust. We evaluated our proposed models on two real-world datasets and the results demonstrate the superior performance of our models compared to the state-of-the-art trust prediction approaches. The experimental results demonstrate that the superior performance of SETTRUST over the three state-of-the-art approaches.

In future works, we will consider other metrics of SET, which exist in real-world relations, like the comparison level or comparison level of alternative, to improve SETTRUST. We plan to consider the time in our social context factors, to be able to deal with real case scenarios such as Fake News. As another line of future work, and to improve the effectiveness which concerns with achieving a high quality result; we plan to use crowdsourcing techniques [6,35]: we will design micro-tasks [7,11] and use the knowledge of the crowd to identify and correct information items that could not be corrected in the proposed algorithms. We plan to offer a domain-model mediated method to use the knowledge of domain experts to identify and correct items that could not be corrected in automatic trust evaluation/detection.

**Acknowledgement.** The corresponding author has been receiving PhD top up scholarship from Data61 since July 2018.

# References

1. Lenhart, A., Purcell, K., Smith, A., Zickuhr, K.: Social Media Mobile Internet Use Among Teens and Young Adults. Millennials. American Life Project, Washington DC (2010)
2. Abu-Salih, B., Wongthongtham, P., Beheshti, S., Zhu, D.: A preliminary approach to domain-based evaluation of users' trustworthiness in online social networks. In: 2015 IEEE International Congress on Big Data, New York City, NY, USA, pp. 460–466 (2015)
3. Beheshti, A., Benatallah, B., Motahari-Nezhad, H.R.: ProcessAtlas: a scalable and extensible platform for business process analytics. Softw. Pract. Exp. **48**(4), 842–866 (2018)
4. Beheshti, A., Benatallah, B., Nouri, R., Chhieng, V.M., Xiong, H., Zhao, X.: CoreDB: a data lake service. In: Proceedings of the 2017 ACM on Conference on Information and Knowledge Management, CIKM 2017, Singapore, 06–10 November 2017, pp. 2451–2454 (2017)

5. Beheshti, A., Benatallah, B., Nouri, R., Tabebordbar, A.: CoreKG: a knowledge lake service. PVLDB **11**(12), 1942–1945 (2018)
6. Beheshti, A., Vaghani, K., Benatallah, B., Tabebordbar, A.: CrowdCorrect: a curation pipeline for social data cleansing and curation. In: Mendling, J., Mouratidis, H. (eds.) CAiSE 2018. LNBIP, vol. 317, pp. 24–38. Springer, Cham (2018). https://doi.org/10.1007/978-3-319-92901-9_3
7. Beheshti, S., Benatallah, B., Motahari-Nezhad, H.R.: Galaxy: a platform for explorative analysis of open data sources. In: Proceedings of the 19th International Conference on Extending Database Technology, EDBT 2016, Bordeaux, France, 15–16 March 2016, pp. 640–643 (2016)
8. Beheshti, S.-M.-R., Benatallah, B., Motahari-Nezhad, H.R., Sakr, S.: A query language for analyzing business processes execution. In: Rinderle-Ma, S., Toumani, F., Wolf, K. (eds.) BPM 2011. LNCS, vol. 6896, pp. 281–297. Springer, Heidelberg (2011). https://doi.org/10.1007/978-3-642-23059-2_22
9. Beheshti, S.-M.-R., et al.: Process Analytics: Concepts and Techniques for Querying and Analyzing Process Data. Springer, Cham (2016). https://doi.org/10.1007/978-3-319-25037-3
10. Beheshti, S., Benatallah, B., Venugopal, S., Ryu, S.H., Motahari-Nezhad, H.R., Wang, W.: A systematic review and comparative analysis of cross-document coreference resolution methods and tools. Computing **99**(4), 313–349 (2017)
11. Beheshti, S., Tabebordbar, A., Benatallah, B., Nouri, R.: On automating basic data curation tasks. In: Proceedings of the 26th International Conference on World Wide Web Companion, Perth, Australia, 3–7 April 2017, pp. 165–169 (2017)
12. Beigi, G., Tang, J., Wang, S., Liu, H.: Exploiting emotional information for trust/distrust prediction. In: Venkatasubramanian, S.C., Meira Jr., W. (eds.) Proceedings of the 2016 SIAM International Conference on Data Mining, USA, pp. 81–89. SIAM (2016)
13. Ding, C., Li, T., Jordan, M.I.: Nonnegative matrix factorization for combinatorial optimization. In: International Conference on Data Mining ICDM, Italy, pp. 183–192 (2008)
14. Sumner, C., Byers, A., Boovhever, R., Park, G.J.: Predicting dark triad personality traits from Twitter usage and a linguistic analysis of tweets. In: 11th International Conference on Machine Learning and Applications, ICMLA, USA, pp. 386–393 (2012)
15. Chen, S.D., Chen, Y., Han, J., Moulin, P.: A feature-enhanced ranking-based classifier for multimodal data and heterogeneous information networks. In: IEEE 13th International Conference on Data Mining, USA, pp. 997–1002 (2013)
16. Dunbar, R.I.M., Clark, A., Hurst, N.L.: Conflict and cooperation among the Vikings: contigent behavioural decisions. Ethol. Sociobiol. **16**, 233 (1995)
17. Blau, P.M.: Exchange and power in social life. Soc. Forces **44**(1), 128 (1965)
18. Liu, G., et al.: Context-aware trust network extraction in large-scale trust-oriented social networks. World Wide Web **21**(3), 713 (2017)
19. Liu, G., Wang, Y., Orgun, M.A.: Social context-aware trust network discovery in complex contextual social networks. In: Proceedings of the 26 AAAI Conference, Canada (2012)
20. Golbeck, J.: Using trust and provenance for content filtering on the semantic web. In: Proceedings of the Workshop on Models of Trust on the Web, at the 15th WWW Conference (2006)
21. Liu, H., et al.: Predicting trusts among users of online communities: an epinions case study. In: EC, pp. 310–319 (2008)

22. Homans, G.C.: Social behavior as exchange. Am. J. Sociol. **63**(6), 597 (1958)
23. Tang, J., Gao, H., Liu, H.: mtrust: discerning multi-faceted trust in a connected world. In: Proceedings of the Fifth WSDM, USA, pp. 93–102 (2012)
24. Tang, J., Gao, H., Hu, X., Liu, H.: Exploiting homophily effect for trust prediction. In: International Conference on Web Search and Data Mining, WSDM, Italy, pp. 53–62 (2013)
25. Jang, M.H., Faloutsos, C., Kim, S.W.: Trust prediction using positive, implicit, and negative information. In: Proceedings of the 23rd International Conference on World Wide Web, WWW 2014 Companion, USA, pp. 303–304 (2014)
26. Uddin, M.G., Zulkernine, M., Ahamed, S.I.: Cat: a context-aware trust model for open and dynamic systems. In: Proceedings of ACM Symposium on Applied Computing (SAC), pp. 2024–2029 (2008)
27. Maamar, Z., Sakr, S., Barnawi, A., Beheshti, S.-M.-R.: A framework of enriching business processes life-cycle with tagging information. In: Sharaf, M.A., Cheema, M.A., Qi, J. (eds.) ADC 2015. LNCS, vol. 9093, pp. 309–313. Springer, Cham (2015). https://doi.org/10.1007/978-3-319-19548-3_25
28. Mayer, R.C., et al.: An integrative model of organizational trust. Acad. Manage. Rev. **20**(3), 709 (1995)
29. Nowell, D.L., Kleinberg, J.M.: The link-prediction problem for social networks. JASIST **58**, 1019 (2007)
30. Guha, R., Kumar, R., Raghavan, P., Tomkins, A.: Propagation of trust and distrust. In: Proceedings of the 13th International Conference on World Wide Web (WWW 2004), pp. 403–412 (2004)
31. Ghafari, S.M., Yakhchi, S., Beheshti, A., Orgun, M.: Social context-aware trust prediction: methods for identifying fake news. In: Hacid, H., Cellary, W., Wang, H., Paik, H.-Y., Zhou, R. (eds.) WISE 2018. LNCS, vol. 11233, pp. 161–177. Springer, Cham (2018). https://doi.org/10.1007/978-3-030-02922-7_11
32. Sanadhya, S., Singh, S.: Trust calculation with ant colony optimization in online social networks. Procedia Comput. Sci. **54**, 186 (2015)
33. Surma, J.: Social exchange in online social networks: the reciprocity phenomenon on Facebook. Comput. Commun. **73**, 342–346 (2016)
34. T. Althoff, P.J., Leskovec, J.: Online actions with offline impact: how online social networks influence online and offline user behavior. In: Proceedings of the Tenth ACM International Conference on Web Search and Data Mining, WSDM, United Kingdom, pp. 537–546 (2017)
35. Tabebordbar, A., Beheshti, A.: Adaptive rule monitoring system. In: Proceedings of the 1st International Workshop on Software Engineering for Cognitive Services, SE4COG@ICSE 2018, Gothenburg, Sweden, 28–29 May 2018, pp. 45–51 (2018)
36. Tang, J., Liu, H.: Trust in social media. Synthesis Lectures on Information Security. Priv. Trust **10**, 1–29 (2015)
37. Thibaut, J., Kelley, H.: The Social Psychology of Groups. Wiley, New York (1959)
38. Zheng, X., Wang, Y., Orgun, M.A., Liu, G., Zhang, H.: Social context-aware trust prediction in social networks. In: Franch, X., Ghose, A.K., Lewis, G.A., Bhiri, S. (eds.) ICSOC 2014. LNCS, vol. 8831, pp. 527–534. Springer, Heidelberg (2014). https://doi.org/10.1007/978-3-662-45391-9_45
39. Wang, Y., Wang, X., Tang, J., Zuo, W., Cai, G.: Modeling status theory in trust prediction. In: Twenty-Ninth AAAI Conference on Artificial Intelligence, USA, pp. 1875–1881 (2015)
40. Wang, Y., Li, L., Liu, G.: Social context-aware trust inference for trust enhancement in social network based recommendations on service providers. World Wide Web **18**, 159 (2015)

# CNR: Cross-network Recommendation Embedding User's Personality

Shahpar Yakhchi$^{(\boxtimes)}$, Seyed Mohssen Ghafari, and Amin Beheshti

Macquarie University, Sydney, Australia
{Shahpar.Yakhchi,seyed-mohssen.ghafari}@hdr.mq.edu.au,
amin.beheshti@mq.edu.au

**Abstract.** With the explosive growth of available data, recommender systems have become an essential tool to ease users with their decision-making procedure. One of the most challenging problems in these systems is the data sparsity problem, i.e., lack of sufficient amount of available users' interactions data. Recently, cross-network recommender systems with the idea of integrating users' activities from multiple domain were presented as a successful solution to address this problem. However, most of the existing approaches utilize users' past behaviour to discover users' preferences on items' patterns and then suggest similar items to them in the future. Hence, their performance may be limited due to ignore recommending divers items. Users are more willing to be recommended with a variety set of items not similar to those they preferred before. Therefore, diversity plays a crucial role to evaluate the recommendation quality. For instance, users who used to watch *comedy* movie, may be less likely to receive *thriller* movie, leading to redundant type of items and decreasing user's satisfaction. In this paper, we aim to exploit user's personality type and incorporate it as a primary and enduring domain-independent factor which has a strong correlation with user's preferences. We present a novel technique and an algorithm to capture users' personality type implicitly without getting users' feedback (e.g., filling questionnaires). We integrate this factor into matrix factorization model and demonstrate the effectiveness of our approach, using a real-world dataset.

**Keywords:** Recommender system · Cross-network recommendation · Personality · Collaborative filtering

## 1 Introduction

With the increasing growth of online information, recommender systems have become an essential tool to efficiently manage this information and ease users with their decision-making procedure [27,28,48,53]. The main purpose of several e-commerce platforms, such as Amazon, Last.fm and Netflix is to monitor users' behavior (e.g., likes, ratings, comments) to understand the user preference on a set of items and use this information to recommend related items that match with users' interests.

© Springer Nature Switzerland AG 2019
H. Hacid et al. (Eds.): QUAT 2018, LNCS 11235, pp. 62–77, 2019.
https://doi.org/10.1007/978-3-030-19143-6_5

Matrix Factorization (MF) is one of the most successful collaborative filtering approaches in single domain recommender systems which have been widely adopted in the literature [37]. MF tries to learn latent vector of user-item interactions and realize users' interests on an unseen item. In this context, data sparsity can be a challenging problem. An example would be in a single domain scenario, when the limited number of users' interactions are available and they are not able to capture users' preferences comprehensively subsequently [30].

In real world, users may use different systems for different reasons. For example, users might prefer to use their Facebook account in order to make a new friend or choose LinkedIn for their business purposes, and choose Netflix to watch videos. Aggregation of these activities on different domains provides an opportunity to understand users' behavior properly and generating cross-network recommendation. In particular, cross-network recommendations have emerged as a solution to cope with the long-standing data sparsity problem [47]. These systems are able to monitor users' behaviors on multiple domains and discover users' preferences completely; thus, improve the recommendation accuracy [31]. Although cross-network recommender systems have shown a great improvement to tackle the data sparsity problem, their performance is limited due to some difficulties. They assume that users' preferences on items are likely to be constant over a period of time and provide users with similar items to those they preferred in the past, degrading recommendations diversity.

For instance, during the Olympic games, a user may be interested to watch wrestling matches on YouTube, expanding new interests. After Olympic, however, the user may have no further interest on wrestling videos and prefer to watch other types of videos. Accordingly, users' preferences may change over time and therefore, there is a need for new approaches to analyze and understand the personality and behavior of users over time. This in turn will create an environment for users to get recommendations with a various set of interesting and unexpected items and can increase users' satisfaction, business profit and loyalty.

To achieve this goal, in this paper, we propose a novel approach to detect users' personality type implicitly, without any burden on users and incorporate it into matrix factorization in order to identify users' interests completely and broaden users' suggestions.

The rest of the paper is organized as follows: Sect. 2 presents the related work. We present an overview and the framework of the proposed approach in Sect. 3. In Sect. 4, we present the results of the evaluation of the proposed approach, before concluding the paper with remarks for future directions in Sect. 5.

## 2  Related Work

### 2.1  Recommender Systems (RSs)

**Recommender Systems** are known as techniques which help both users and companies. Their aim is to assist customers with decision-making procedure to find interesting items matching with their preferences. The growing number of available digital information and due to increasing popularity of visitors to the Internet create the information overload problem. Therefore, systems such as Google have appeared to deal with this problem and help users to discover their interested items. Here, there is an increasing need for system to solve this problem and assist users has emerged. Recommender systems have known as an information filtering systems which mitigate information overload problem by filtering crucial information from all collected information [2]. Recommender system trace user's actions and history and collect information preferred items and rating pattern to predict which items are more likely to prefer in the future.

Recommender systems can be beneficial to both providers and customers. There are various reasons why recommender systems attract providers' attention; firstly it can boost sales rate which can be an essential reason for service providers to recommend items with the highest possibility of acceptance, secondly suggest different items where might not be achieved without recommender system in which captures user's interest and finally increase loyalty and user's satisfaction. In user's point of view, they are eased with their decision-making procedure as recommender systems filter their desired and interesting items to them. There are five different type of recommender systems in the literature which have been investigated widely [22].

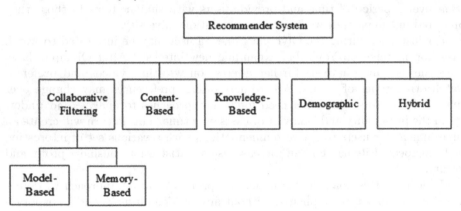

**Content-Based.** Recommending items similar to those that a user likes before, say in movie recommender, if the user watched and liked a drama genre movie, another drama one will be recommended to this user. The main goal of content-based recommender system is to find items in which attributes are similar to users' profile [41]. In order to discover similarity between items there are different either statistical analysis such as Naïve Bayes Classifier [26] or machine learning techniques like Decision Trees [50] or Neural Networks [17]. Item is a general concept which regarding to the recommender system suggestions can be CD, Movie, Book and etc.

**Collaborative-Filtering.** Methods belonging to this category can be divided in the two different classes known as memory-based and model-based techniques. Model-based approaches learn the user-item ratings to predict user's interest on an unseen item, including Bayesian Clustering [19], Latent Dirichlet Allocation [18], Support Vector Machines [29] and Singular Value Decomposition [16,36, 54,55]. While methods in Memory-based class use similarity metric to measure similarity either between users or items [25,40].

**Knowledge-Based Recommender** tries to acquire knowledge about domain from users to make recommendation more accurate [59]. These systems explicitly ask user's preferences and then make an appropriate recommendation.

**Demographic-Based Recommender** aim to find demographic information about users such as age, nationality, gender to provide a better recommendation which suits user's interests [39,45].

**Hybrid** approaches merge mentioned techniques together to benefit from their advantages in one model [21].

Data sparsity is one of the shortcoming that Collaborative Filtering (CF) approaches are confronted with. Some works such as CTR integrates topic molding to use additional information like the contents of documents to make a recommendation [60] and TopicMF which not only uses ratings but also exploits review texts to discover more data from them [5]. Although resorting to extra information can create an environment for recommendation systems to better understand users' preferences, but they might be infeasible in the real-world scenarios. In order to understand users' preferences completely, some other studies provide a questionnaire for users to directly ask their interests on different items [49]. The major difficulty of these kinds of approach is that users may avoid to participate in filling a questionnaire as it is a time consuming task.

In contrast to recommender systems on single domain, cross-network approaches appear to mitigate data sparsity problem and improve recommendation accuracy. They enrich data and generate accurate user profile with the help of auxiliary domain [44]. Although, widely attempts have been done in the literature to alleviate the data sparsity problem, diversity is a key factor that has been neglected in the most of them (Table 1).

**Table 1.** Big five factor features

| Big five factor model | Features |
| --- | --- |
| Openness | Fantasy aesthetics feeling actions |
| Neuroticism | Anxiety angry hostility depression |
| Conscientiousness | Competence order deliberation |
| Extraversion | Activity excitement-seeking warmth positive emotions |
| Agreeableness | Trust straightforwardness altruism compliance |

## 2.2 What Is Personality?

Personality was explained as "consistent behavior pattern and interpersonal processes originating within the individual" [20]. From psychological point of view, people differ in their behaviours and attitudes, which can be explained by their personality type. Personality is a stable feature without no changes over time. In terms of psychological view, there are different personality traits which among all Five Factor Model (FFM) is "the dominant paradigm in personality research and one of the most influential models in all of the psychology" [42]. The Big Five structure does not imply that Personality differences can be reduced to only five traits. Yet, these five dimensions represent Personality at the broadest level of abstraction, and each dimension summarizes a large number of distinct, more specific Personality characteristics" [34]. FFM has five principal dimensions Openness to experience, Conscientiousness, Extraversion, Agreeableness, Neuroticism (OCEAN). As it is clear from Table 3, FFM are accompanied with different features;

### 2.3 Personality and User's Preferences

It is conducted that our personality type plays an important role in our preferences on music, movies, TV shows, books and magazines [52]. This correlation provides an opportunity for RSs to suggest a divers set of items to users. To extract personality, Linguistic Inquiry and Word Count (LIWC) tool is a successful platform to identify 88 categories of linguistic features relevant to each domain of the FFM [56]. Research findings confirm that there is a strong correlation between personality type and user's preferences in various fields, like music [33] books and magazines [51].

### 2.4 Personality Recognition

Personality is a domain-independent and stable factor that can be extracted explicitly *i.e., questionnaire* or implicitly. In order to find personality type implicitly, we can analyze user's behaviours, actions like posts, comments and etc. Moreover, by analyzing digital or language-based features of written texts we will unable to predict user's personality type implicitly with no need to user effort [4]. While explicit personality detection is more easier, it is time-consuming task and participants might be unwilling to attend due to privacy concern. In this type of personality recognition, individuals are asked to answer questions regarding to specific psychological personality model. Below we list the popular questionnaire regarding to the Big Five Factors [57]:

- 240-items NEO-PI-R [43];
- 300-items NEO-IPIP [35];
- 100-items FFPI [1];
- 132-items BFQ [6];
- 120-items SIFFM [58];

We detect the user's personality type implicitly with the help of Linguistic Inquiry and Word Count (LIWC) tool to understand how many words of users' reviews are related to each category of this tool. Below, we represent LIWC categorize based on the [46] (Fig. 1):

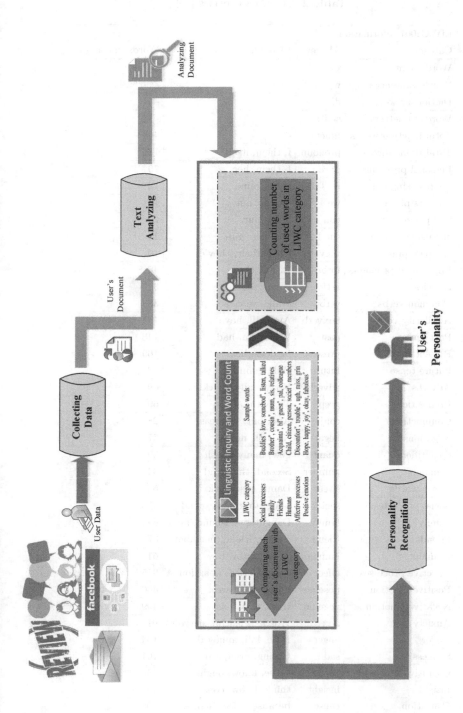

**Fig. 1.** Personality detection

**Table 2.** LIWC categorizes [46]

| LIWC2007 information | | | |
|---|---|---|---|
| Category | Abbrev | Examples | Words in category |
| Word count | wc | - | - |
| Words/sentences | wps | - | - |
| Dictionary words | dic | - | - |
| Words >6 letters | sixltr | - | - |
| Total function words | funct | - | 464 |
| Total pronounce | pronoun | I, them, itself | 116 |
| Personal pronouns | ppron | I, them, her | 70 |
| 1st pers singular | i | I, me, mine | 12 |
| 1st pers plural | we | We, us, our | 12 |
| 2nd person | you | You, your | 20 |
| 3rd pers singular | she he | She, her, him | 17 |
| 3rd pers plural | they | They, their, they'd | 10 |
| Impersonal pronouns | ipron | It, it's, those | 46 |
| Articles | article | A, an, the | 3 |
| Common verbs | verb | Walk, went, see | 383 |
| Auxilarity verbs | auxverb | Am, will, have | 144 |
| Past tense | past | Went, ran, had | 145 |
| Present tense | present | Is, does, hear | 169 |
| Future tense | future | Will, gonna | 48 |
| Adverbs | adverb | Very, really, quickly | 69 |
| Prepositions | prep | To, with, above | 60 |
| Conjunctions | conj | And, but, whereas | 28 |
| Negations | negate | No, not, never | 57 |
| Quantifiers | quant | Few, many, much | 89 |
| Numbers | number | Second, thousand | 34 |
| Swear words | swear | Damn, piss, fuck | 53 |
| Social processes | social | Mate, talk, they, child | 455 |
| Family | family | Daughter, husband, aunt | 64 |
| Friends | friend | Buddy, friend, neighbor | 37 |
| Humans | human | Adult, baby, boy | 61 |
| Affective processes | affect | Happy, cried, abandon | 915 |
| Positive emotion | posemo | Love, nice, sweet | 406 |
| Negative emotion | negemo | Hurt, ugly, nasty | 499 |
| Anxiety | anx | Worried, fearful, nervous | 91 |
| Anger | anger | Hate, kill, annoyed | 184 |
| Sadness | sad | Crying, grief, sad | 101 |
| Cognitive processes | cogmech | cause, know, ought | 730 |
| Insight | insight | think, know, consider | 195 |
| Causation | cause | because, effect, hence | 108 |

**Table 2.** (*continued*)

| LIWC2007 information | | | |
|---|---|---|---|
| Category | Abbrev | Examples | Words in category |
| Discrepancy | discrep | should, would, could | 76 |
| Tentative | tentat | maybe, perhaps, guess | 155 |
| Certainty | certain | always, never | 83 |
| Inhibition | inhib | block, constrain, stop | 111 |
| Inclusive | incl | And, with, include | 18 |
| Exclusive | excl | But, without, exclude | 17 |
| Perceptual processes | percept | Observing, heard, feeling | 273 |
| See | see | View, saw, seen | 72 |
| Hear | hear | Listen, hearing | 51 |
| Feel | feel | Feels, touch | 75 |
| Biological processes | bio | Eat, blood, pain | 567 |
| Body | body | Cheek, hands, spit | 180 |
| Health | health | Clinic, flu, pill | 236 |
| Sexual | sexual | Horny, love, incest | 96 |
| Ingestion | ingest | Dish, eat, pizza | 111 |
| Relativity | relativ | Area, bend, exit, stop | 638 |
| Motion | motion | Arrive, car, go | 168 |
| Space | space | Down, in, thin | 220 |
| Time | time | End, until, season | 239 |
| Work | work | Job, majors, xerox | 327 |
| Achievement | achieve | Earn, hero, win | 186 |
| Leisure | leisure | Cook, chat, movie | 229 |
| Home | home | Apartment, kitchen, family | 93 |
| Money | money | Audit, cash, owe | 173 |
| Religion | relig | Altar, church, mosque | 159 |
| Death | death | Bury, coffin, kill | 62 |
| Assent | assent | Agree, OK, yes | 30 |
| Nonfluencies | nonflu | Er, hm, umm | 8 |
| Fillers | filler | Blah, Imean, youknow | 9 |

# 3 Methodology

## 3.1 Preliminary Knowledge

Assume we have $K$ items $V = \{v_1, v_2, \cdots, v_K\}$, and $L$ users $U = \{u_1, u_2, \cdots, u_L\}$ and $R \in \mathbb{R}^{K \times L}$ is the rating matrix, and $R_{ij}$ indicates ratings which have been given to item $i$ by user $j$. Let $W \in \mathbb{R}^{N \times N}$ represents the personality matrix, where $W_{ij} = \{0, 1\}$, and when $W_{ij} = 1$ it means that users $u_i$ and $u_j$ have a similar personality type.

## 3.2   Our Model

$R_{ij}$ predicts the value for unrated items which user $u_i$ will give to item $v_j$;

$$R_{ij} = p_i^T q_j \tag{1}$$

Where $p_i$ and $q_j$ are latent feature vector for user $i$ and item $j$ respectively,

$$min \frac{1}{2} \sum_{i=1}^{O} \sum_{j=1}^{L} I_{ij} \left( R_{ij} - \left( \gamma p_i^T q_j + \left( (1-\gamma) \sum_{t \in \theta_i^+} W_{it} p_t^T q_j \right) \right) \right)^2$$
$$+ \alpha_1 \|P\|_F^2 + \alpha_2 \|Q\|_F^2 \tag{2}$$

In the above equation, $I_{ij} = 1$, if user $i$ has rated item $j$, otherwise $I_{ij} = 0$. Matrix $W$ contains personality information, and $\theta i_i^+$ is the set of users who are in the same personality type network with user $i$, and $\beta$ is a controlling parameter to control the weight of user's preferences. To save space, we omit the detailed of the updating rules.

**Table 3.** Datasets statistics

| | |
|---|---|
| Number of users | 2000 |
| Number of items | 1500 |
| Number of reviews | 86690 |
| User ratings density | 0.0024 |
| Average number of rates per user | 3.6113 |
| Average number of rates per item | 0.2166 |
| Number of rated items | 7219 |

# 4   Experimental Settings and Analysis

## 4.1   Datasets and Evaluation

We have selected Amazon dataset, which consists of a large number of reviews. In this paper, we have used Amazon Instant-video, because of its high relation between user's preferences on video and their personality types and leave other domains for cross-network recommender as our future works. The dataset includes 2000 users who wrote more than 3 reviews.

**Evaluation.** We select two popular evaluation metrics, Mean Square Error (MSE) and Root Mean Squared Error (RMSE);

$$MAE = \frac{\sum_{(u,i) \in R_{test}} | \hat{R}_{ui} - R_{ui} |}{| R_{test} |}, \tag{3}$$

$$RMSE = \sqrt{\frac{\sum_{(u,i) \in R_{test}} |\hat{R}_{ui} - R_{ui}|}{|R_{test}|}} \tag{4}$$

where, $R_{ui}$ and $\hat{R}_{ui}$ are real and predicted ratings values respectively, and $R_{test}$ represents the user-item in the test dataset.

In order to comparison, we select SVD++, a single model in which integrates both neighborhood and latent factor approaches [36], Hu which proposes a metric to use of user personality characteristics and rating information [32] and Random model (Figs. 2 and 3).

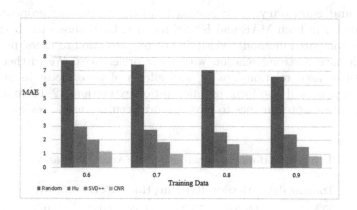

**Fig. 2.** MAE comparison

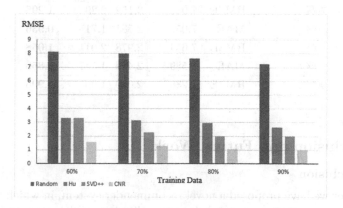

**Fig. 3.** RMSE comparison

## 4.2   Performance Comparison and Analysis

As it can be seen from Table 2, we use different sets of the training data size (60%, 70%, 80%, 90%), when we increased the size of training dataset the performance of all methods was improved. Therefore, to have a fair comparison, we consider the results related to 90% training size. Our proposed model, CNR, shows the best performance in terms of both RMSE and MAE among all approaches. The performance of CNR is improved compared to the SVD++ by 64%, 50% in terms of MAE and RMSE respectively and SVD++ performs around 2 and 6 times better compared to the Hu and Random methods in both evaluation metrics.

**Analysis and Summary.** As it is clear from the results our proposed model performs better in both MAE and RMSE metrics. CNR shows the best performance over compared methods, which do not pay attention to users' personality type which have a strong relation with their preferences. We further investigate the time-based relationships [7] and effects of time factor in our future works. Finally, we will also focus on Information extraction [12–14] and Natural language processing techniques to have a more accurate users' reviews analysis (Table 4).

**Table 4.** Performance analysis on the Amazon dataset

| Training data | Metrics | Random | Hu | SVD++ | CNR |
|---|---|---|---|---|---|
| 60% | MAE | 7.759 | 2.983 | 2.033 | 1.165 |
| 60% | RMSE | 8.124 | 3.32 | 2.314 | 1.554 |
| 70% | MAE | 7.467 | 2.763 | 1.864 | 1.005 |
| 70% | RMSE | 7.985 | 3.152 | 2.29 | 1.295 |
| 80% | MAE | 7.058 | 2.581 | 1.71 | 0.936 |
| 80% | RMSE | 7.654 | 2.978 | 2.011 | 1.058 |
| 90% | MAE | 6.589 | 2.426 | 1.547 | 0.850 |
| 90% | RMSE | 7.236 | 2.649 | 1.99 | 0.995 |

# 5   Conclusion and Future Work

## 5.1   Conclusion

In this paper we have proposed a novel recommender system, in which exploiting user's written reviews to discover their personality type which plays an important role in users' decision-making process. Extensive validation on Amazon dataset demonstrates the advantages of our approach compared to the other methods in terms of both RMSE and MAE. In our future work, we will discover users' personality characteristics and make a recommendation in separate domains to have a cross-domain recommendation. Furthermore, according to the Sect. 4.2, CNR is able to recommend divers set of items to users.

## 5.2 Future Work : Behavioural Analytics and Recommender Systems

Behavioural Analytics, a recent advancement in business analytics that focuses on providing insight into the actions of people, has the potential to enable Recommender Systems understanding the personality, behaviour and attitude of its users and come up with more accurate and timely recommendations. As an ongoing and future work, we plan to:

- link Behavioural Analytics and Recommender Systems by collecting the activities of Recommender Systems users. We will introduce the new notion of Behavioural Provenance [11,15], to be able to trace the user activities back to their origin and provide evidences to understand the personality, behaviour and attitude of Recommender Systems users.
- transform the collected (raw) user activity data into contextualized Behavioural data and knowledge. We will use our previous work, Knowledge Lake [8,9] to automatically curate the Behaviour data and provenance, and to prepare it for analytics and reasoning.
- introduce a new generation of smart Recommender Systems, by leveraging the advances in natural language processing [14] machine learning [3] and crowdsourcing [10], to leverage the contextualized data and knowledge (generated in previous steps), and to provide cognitive assistant to the Recommender System users.

# References

1. Jolijn Hendrinks, A.A., Hofstee, W.B.K., De Raad, B.: The five-factor personality inventory: assessing the big five by means of brief and concrete statements, pp. 79–108 (2002)
2. Aciar, S., Zhang, D., Simoff, S.J., Debenham, J.K.: Informed recommender: basing recommendations on consumer product reviews. IEEE Intell. Syst. **22**(3), 39–47 (2007)
3. Amouzgar, F., Beheshti, A., Ghodratnama, S., Benatallah, B., Yang, J., Sheng, Q.Z.: isheets: a spreadsheet-based machine learning development platform for data-driven process analytics. In: 2018 The 16th International Conference on Service-Oriented Computing (ICSOC), HangZhou, China (2018)
4. Azaria, A., Hong, J.: Recommender systems with personality. In: Proceedings of the 10th ACM Conference on Recommender Systems, Boston, 15–19 September 2016, pp. 207–210 (2016)
5. Bao, Y., Fang, H., Zhang, J.: Topicmf: simultaneously exploiting ratings and reviews for recommendation. In: Proceedings of the Twenty-Eighth AAAI Conference on Artificial Intelligence, Québec City, Québec, Canada, 27–31 July 2014, pp. 2–8 (2014)
6. Barbaranelli, C., Caprara, G.V.: Studies of the big five questionnaire, pp. 109–128 (2002)
7. Beheshti, A., Benatallah, B., Motahari-Nezhad, H.R.: Processatlas: a scalable and extensible platform for business process analytics. Softw. Pract. Exper. **48**, 842–866 (2018)

8. Beheshti, A., Benatallah, B., Nouri, R., Chhieng, V.M., Xiong, H., Zhao, X.: Coredb: a data lake service. In: Proceedings of the 2017 ACM on Conference on Information and Knowledge Management, CIKM 2017, Singapore, 06–10 November 2017, pp. 2451–2454 (2017). https://doi.org/10.1145/3132847.3133171

9. Beheshti, A., Benatallah, B., Nouri, R., Tabebordbar, A.: Corekg: a knowledge lake service. PVLDB **11**(12), 1942–1945 (2018). http://www.vldb.org/pvldb/vol11/p1942-beheshti.pdf

10. Beheshti, A., Vaghani, K., Benatallah, B., Tabebordbar, A.: CrowdCorrect: a curation pipeline for social data cleansing and curation. In: Mendling, J., Mouratidis, H. (eds.) CAiSE 2018. LNBIP, vol. 317, pp. 24–38. Springer, Cham (2018). https://doi.org/10.1007/978-3-319-92901-9_3

11. Beheshti, S.-M.-R., Benatallah, B., Motahari-Nezhad, H.R.: Enabling the analysis of cross-cutting aspects in ad-hoc processes. In: Salinesi, C., Norrie, M.C., Pastor, Ó. (eds.) CAiSE 2013. LNCS, vol. 7908, pp. 51–67. Springer, Heidelberg (2013). https://doi.org/10.1007/978-3-642-38709-8_4

12. Beheshti, S.-M.-R., Benatallah, B., Motahari-Nezhad, H.R., Sakr, S.: A query language for analyzing business processes execution. In: Rinderle-Ma, S., Toumani, F., Wolf, K. (eds.) BPM 2011. LNCS, vol. 6896, pp. 281–297. Springer, Heidelberg (2011). https://doi.org/10.1007/978-3-642-23059-2_22

13. Beheshti, S.-M.-R., et al.: Process Analytics - Concepts and Techniques for Querying and Analyzing Process Data. Springer, Cham (2016). https://doi.org/10.1007/978-3-319-25037-3

14. Beheshti, S.M.R., Benatallah, B., Venugopal, S., Ryu, S.H., Motahari-Nezhad, H.R., Wang, W.: A systematic review and comparative analysis of cross-document coreference resolution methods and tools. Computing **99**(4), 313–349 (2017). https://doi.org/10.1007/s00607-016-0490-0

15. Beheshti, S-M-R., Nezhad, H.R.M., Benatallah, B.: Temporal provenance model (TPM): model and query language. CoRR abs/1211.5009, http://arxiv.org/abs/1211.5009 (2012)

16. Bell, R.M., Koren, Y., Volinsky, C.: Modeling relationships at multiple scales to improve accuracy of large recommender systems. In: Proceedings of the 13th ACM SIGKDD International Conference on Knowledge Discovery and Data Mining, San Jose, California, USA, 12–15 August 2007, pp. 95–104 (2007)

17. Bishop, C.M.: Pattern Recognition and Machine Learning. Information science and statistics, 5th edn. Springer, Boston (2007). https://doi.org/10.1007/978-1-4615-7566-5

18. Blei, D.M., Ng, A.Y., Jordan, M.I.: Latent Dirichlet allocation. J. Mach. Learn. Res. **3**, 993–1022 (2003)

19. Breese, J.S., Heckerman, D., Kadie, C.M.: Empirical analysis of predictive algorithms for collaborative filtering. CoRR abs/1301.7363 (2013)

20. Burger, J.M.: Introduction to personality (2011)

21. Burke, R.D.: Hybrid recommender systems: survey and experiments. User Model. User-Adapt. Interact. **12**(4), 331–370 (2002)

22. Burke, R.: Hybrid web recommender systems. In: Brusilovsky, P., Kobsa, A., Nejdl, W. (eds.) The Adaptive Web. LNCS, vol. 4321, pp. 377–408. Springer, Heidelberg (2007). https://doi.org/10.1007/978-3-540-72079-9_12

23. Cantador, I., Fernández-Tobías, I., Bellogín, A.: Relating personality types with user preferences in multiple entertainment domains. In: Late-Breaking Results, Project Papers and Workshop Proceedings of the 21st Conference on User Modeling, Adaptation, and Personalization, Rome, Italy, 10–14 June 2013 (2013)

24. Davidson, J., et al.: The Youtube video recommendation system. In: Proceedings of the fourth ACM Conference on Recommender Systems, pp. 293–296 (2010)
25. Deshpande, M., Karypis, G.: Item-based top-N recommendation algorithms. ACM Trans. Inf. Syst. **22**(1), 143–177 (2004)
26. Friedman, N., Geiger, D., Goldszmidt, M.: Bayesian network classifiers. Mach. Learn. **29**(2–3), 131–163 (1997)
27. Ghafari, S.M., Yakhchi, S., Beheshti, A., Orgun, M.: Social context-aware trust prediction: methods for identifying fake news. In: Hacid, H., Cellary, W., Wang, H., Paik, H.-Y., Zhou, R. (eds.) WISE 2018. LNCS, vol. 11233, pp. 161–177. Springer, Cham (2018). https://doi.org/10.1007/978-3-030-02922-7_11
28. Gomez-Uribe, C.A., Hunt, N.: The Netflix recommender system: algorithms, business value, and innovation. ACM Trans. Manag. Inf. Syst. (TMIS) **6**(4), 13 (2016)
29. Grčar, M., Fortuna, B., Mladenič, D., Grobelnik, M.: kNN versus SVM in the collaborative filtering framework. In: Batagelj, V., Bock, H.H., Ferligoj, A., Žiberna, A. (eds.) Data Science and Classification. Studies in Classification, Data Analysis, and Knowledge Organization. Springer, Heidelberg (2006). https://doi.org/10.1007/3-540-34416-0_27
30. He, X., Chua, T.: Neural factorization machines for sparse predictive analytics. In: Proceedings of the 40th International ACM SIGIR Conference on Research and Development in Information Retrieval, Shinjuku, Tokyo, Japan, 7–11 August 2017, pp. 355–364 (2017)
31. He, X., Zhang, H., Kan, M., Chua, T.: Fast matrix factorization for online recommendation with implicit feedback. CoRR abs/1708.05024 (2017)
32. Hu, R., Pu, P.: Enhancing collaborative filtering systems with personality information. In: Proceedings of the 2011 ACM Conference on Recommender Systems, RecSys 2011, Chicago, IL, USA, 23–27 October 2011, pp. 197–204 (2011)
33. IRentfrow, P.J., Goldberg, L.R., Zilca, R.: Listening, watching, and reading: the structure and correlates of entertainment preferences. J. Pers. **79**, 223–258 (2011)
34. John, O.P., Srivastava, S.: The big five trait taxonomy: history, measurement, and theoretical perspectives. In: Pervin, L.A., John, O.P. (eds.) Handbook of Personality: Theory and research, pp. 102–138. Guilford Press, New York (1999)
35. Johnson, J.A.: Web-based personality assesment (2000)
36. Koren, Y.: Factorization meets the neighborhood: a multifaceted collaborative filtering model. In: Proceedings of the 14th ACM SIGKDD International Conference on Knowledge Discovery and Data Mining, Las Vegas, Nevada, USA, 24–27 August 2008, pp. 426–434 (2008)
37. Koren, Y., Bell, R.M., Volinsky, C.: Matrix factorization techniques for recommender systems. IEEE Comput. **42**(8), 30–37 (2009)
38. Kosinski, M., Stillwell, D., Graepel, T.: Private traits and attributes are predictable from digital records of human behavior. Proc. Nat. Acad. Sci. **110**, 5802–5805 (2013)
39. Krulwich, B., Burkey, C.: The infofinder agent: learning user interests through heuristic phrase extraction. IEEE Expert **12**(5), 22–27 (1997)
40. Linden, G., Smith, B., York, J.: Amazon.com recommendations: item-to-item collaborative filtering. IEEE Internet Comput. **7**(1), 76–80 (2003)
41. Lops, P., de Gemmis, M., Semeraro, G.: Content-based Recommender systems: state of the art and trends. In: Ricci, F., Rokach, L., Shapira, B., Kantor, P.B. (eds.) Recommender Systems Handbook. LNCS, pp. 73–105. Springer, Boston, MA (2011). https://doi.org/10.1007/978-0-387-85820-3_3
42. McCrae, R.R.: The five-factor model of personality traits: consensus and controversy (2009)

43. McCrae, R.R., John, O.P.: An introduction to the five-factor model and its applications. J. Pers. **60**, 175–216 (1992)

44. Pan, W., Xiang, E.W., Liu, N.N., Yang, Q.: Transfer learning in collaborative filtering for sparsity reduction. In: Proceedings of the Twenty-Fourth AAAI Conference on Artificial Intelligence, AAAI 2010, Atlanta, Georgia, USA, 11–15 July 2010 (2010)

45. Pazzani, M.J.: A framework for collaborative, content-based and demographic filtering. Artif. Intell. Rev. **13**(5–6), 393–408 (1999)

46. Pennebaker, J.W., Francis, M.E., Booth, R.J.: Linguistic inquiry and word count: Liwc **2001**, 71 (2001)

47. Perera, D., Zimmermann, R.: LSTM networks for online cross-network recommendations. In: Proceedings of the Twenty-Seventh International Joint Conference on Artificial Intelligence, IJCAI 2018, Stockholm, Sweden, 13–19 July 2018, pp. 3825–3833 (2018)

48. Posse, C.: Key lessons learned building recommender systems for large-scale social networks. In: Proceedings of the 18th ACM SIGKDD International Conference on Knowledge Discovery and Data Mining, p. 587 (2012)

49. Rashid, A.M., et al.: Getting to know you: learning new user preferences in recommender systems. In: Proceedings of the 7th International Conference on Intelligent User Interfaces, IUI 2002, San Francisco, California, USA, 13–16 January 2002, pp. 127–134 (2002)

50. Rastogi, R., Sharma, S., Chandra, S.: Robust parametric twin support vector machine for pattern classification. Neural Process. Lett. **47**(1), 293–323 (2018)

51. Rentfrow, P.J., Gosling, S.D.: The do re mi's of everyday life: the structure and personality correlates of music preferences. J. Pers. Soc. Psychol. **84**, 1236–1256 (2003)

52. Rentfrow, P.J., Goldberg, L.R., Zilca, R.: Listening, watching, and reading: the structure and correlates of entertainment preferences. J. Pers. **79**(2), 223–258 (2011)

53. Salih, B.A., Wongthongtham, P., Beheshti, S., Zajabbari, B.: Towards a methodology for social business intelligence in the era of big social data incorporating trust and semantic analysis. In: Second International Conference on Advanced Data and Information Engineering (DaEng-2015). Springer, Bali, Indonesia (2015)

54. Takács, G., Pilászy, I., Németh, B., Tikk, D.: Investigation of various matrix factorization methods for large recommender systems. In: Workshops Proceedings of the 8th IEEE International Conference on Data Mining (ICDM 2008), Pisa, Italy, 15–19 December 2008, pp. 553–562 (2008)

55. Takács, G., Pilászy, I., Németh, B., Tikk, D.: Scalable collaborative filtering approaches for large recommender systems. J. Mach. Learn. Res. **10**, 623–656 (2009)

56. Tausczik, Y.R., Pennebaker, J.W.: The psychological meaning of words: Liwc and computerized text analysis methods. J. Lang. Soc. Psychol. **29**(1), 24–54 (2010)

57. Tom Buchanan, J.A.J., Goldberg, L.R.: Implementing a five-factor personality inventory for use on the internet. **21**, 116–128 (2005)

58. Trull, T.J., Widiger, T.A.: The structured interveew for the five factor model of personality, pp. 148–170 (2002)

59. Viktoratos, I., Tsadiras, A., Bassiliades, N.: Combining community-based knowledge with association rule mining to alleviate the cold start problem in context-aware recommender systems. Expert Syst. Appl. **101**, 78–90 (2018). https://doi.org/10.1016/j.eswa.2018.01.044

60. Wang, C., Blei, D.M.: Collaborative topic modeling for recommending scientific articles. In: Proceedings of the 17th ACM SIGKDD International Conference on Knowledge Discovery and Data Mining, San Diego, CA, USA, 21–24 August 2011, pp. 448–456 (2011)

# Firefly Algorithm with Proportional Adjustment Strategy

Jing Wang[1]([⊠]), Guiyuan Liu[1], and William Wei Song[1,2]

[1] School of Software and Internet of Things Engineering,
Jiangxi University of Finance and Economics, Nanchang, China
wangjing@jxufe.edu.cn
[2] Dalarna University, Borlänge, Sweden
wso@du.se

**Abstract.** Firefly algorithm is a new heuristic intelligent optimization algorithm and has excellent performance in many optimization problems. However, in the face of some multimodal and high-dimensional problems, the algorithm is easy to fall into the local optimum. In order to avoid this phenomenon, this paper proposed an improved firefly algorithm with proportional adjustment strategy for alpha and beta. Thirteen well-known benchmark functions are used to verify the performance of our proposed algorithm, the computational results show that our proposed algorithm is more efficient than many other FA algorithms.

**Keywords:** Firefly algorithm · Meta-heuristic algorithm ·
Intelligent optimization algorithm · Global optimization

## 1 Introduction

Firefly algorithm (FA) is a new heuristic optimization algorithm proposed by Yang in 2008 [1] by simulating the phenomenon of real firefly swarm in nature. Compared with other heuristic swarm intelligence optimization algorithms such as Ant Colony Optimization (ACO) and Particle Swarm Optimization (PSO), FA is simple, efficient, and easy to implement and operate, quickly attracts the attention of a large number of researchers, and has been applied to many practical engineering optimization problems [2–5].

However, the firefly algorithm is also faced with the same common problems as other intelligent optimization algorithms, such as being easily trapped in local optimal values, and low accuracy in solving some problems. Therefore, this paper proposes a proportional adjustment strategy for attraction and step size of FA, called proportional firefly algorithm (PFA). Firstly, by changing the initial value of the attraction parameter, the individual firefly can be approached to the better individual firefly in a certain proportion, so as to preserve the spatial diversity of the firefly population and improve the global optimization ability of the algorithm. Secondly, in terms of step size, we design an exponential iterative reduction model of step size and adjust the step size to meet the requirements of different objective functions at different stages of evolution.

© Springer Nature Switzerland AG 2019
H. Hacid et al. (Eds.): QUAT 2018, LNCS 11235, pp. 78–93, 2019.
https://doi.org/10.1007/978-3-030-19143-6_6

The rest of this paper is organized as follows. In the Sect. 2, we introduce the related concepts of standard FA. The Sect. 3 mainly introduces the improvement of FA algorithm by other scholars in recent years. Section 4 presents the PFA algorithm and discusses the steps and ideas of the algorithm in detail. The comparison results between the PFA algorithm and other FA algorithm version is given in the Sect. 4.3. Finally, in the Sect. 5, we summarize the PFA algorithm and discuss the future improvement of PFA algorithm.

## 2    A Brief Review of Firefly Algorithm

There are four very important concepts in the firefly algorithm: light intensity, attractiveness, distance and movement.

**Light Intensity:** The light intensity $I(r)$ is defined by Yang [6]:

$$I(r) = I_0 e^{-\gamma r^2} \tag{1}$$

where $I_0$ is the initial brightness. The parameter $\gamma$ is the light absorption coefficient, $r$ is the distance between two fireflies.

**Attractiveness:** The attractiveness of a firefly is monotonically decreasing as the distance increases, and the attractiveness is defined as follows [6]:

$$\beta(r) = \beta_0 e^{-\gamma r^2} \tag{2}$$

where $\beta_0$ is the attractiveness at $r = 0$. The light absorption coefficient $\gamma$ will determine the variation of attractiveness $\beta$ and $\gamma \in [0, \infty]$. For most practical implementations, Yang suggests that $\gamma = 1$ and $\beta_0 = 1$.

**Distance:** For two fireflies $x_i$ and $x_j$, $r$ is defined by Yang [6]:

$$r_{ij} = \|x_i - x_j\| = \sqrt{\sum_{d=1}^{D}(x_{id} - x_{jd})^2} \tag{3}$$

**Movement:** The light intensity of the weak firefly will move to another brighter firefly, assuming that a firefly $x_j$ is more brighter than firefly $x_i$, the position update equation given by the following formula [6]:

$$x_i(t+1) = x_i(t) + \beta_0 e^{-\gamma r^2}(x_j(t) - x_i(t)) + \alpha\epsilon_i \tag{4}$$

where $t$ is the iterations. The third term of the right is a random disturbance term which contains $\alpha$ and $\epsilon_i$, $\alpha \in [0, 1]$ is the step factor, $\epsilon_i \in [0.5, 0.5]$ is a random number vector obtained by Gaussian distribution or Levy flight [7].

The framework of standard FA is listed below, FEs is the number of evaluations, *MAXFEs* is the maximum number of evaluations, and PS is the population size.

| **Algorithm 1:** Framework of FA |
|---|
| 1      Randomly initialize $N$ fireflies (solutions) as an initial population   $\{X_i \mid i = 1, 2, ..., N\}$; |
| 2      Calculate the fitness v of each firefly $X_i$; |
| 3      FEs = 0 and PS = $N$; |
| 4      **while** *this* $\leq$ *MAXFEs* |
| 5         **for** *i*= 1 to *N* |
| 6             **for** *j* = 1 to *N* |
| 7                if $f(X_j) < f(X_i)$ |
| 8                    Move $X_i$ towards $X_j$ according to Eq. 4; |
| 9                    Calculate the fitness value of the new $X_i$; |
| 10                    FEs++; |
| 11                **end if** |
| 12             **end for** |
| 13         **end for** |
| 14      **end while** |

In the standard glowworm optimization algorithm, the location update of fireflies is mainly based on the attraction of fireflies and the disturbance step in the movement of fireflies themselves. In order to balance their relationship, many scholars have done a lot of research on adjusting the step parameters of the random movement of fireflies and the attraction step parameters of fireflies. Fister et al. [8] proposed a memetic self-adaptive FA (MFA), where values of control parameters are changed during the run. Experimental results show that MFA were very promising and showed a potential that this algorithm could successfully be applied in near future to the other combinatorial optimization.

MFA makes the dynamic change of the step factor with the evolutionary iteration. It is redefined as follows:

$$\alpha(t+1) = \left(\frac{1}{9000}\right)^{\frac{1}{t}} \alpha(t), \tag{5}$$

where $t$ represents the current iteration. In the above-mentioned MFA [8], Fister also changes the fireflies' movement strategy, which can be defined by the following equation:

$$x_{id}(t+1) = x_{id}(t) + \beta(x_{jd}(t) - x_{id}(t)) + \alpha(t)s_d\epsilon_i, \tag{6}$$

where

$$\beta = \beta_{min} + (\beta_0 - \beta_{min})e^{-\gamma r^2},\tag{7}$$

$$s_d = x_d^{max} - x_d^{min},\tag{8}$$

$x_{id}$ denotes the $d$-dimensional variable of the $i$-th firefly, $\beta_{min}$ is usually set to 0.2 that is the minimum value in $\beta$, $s_d$ is the length of the domain of the initialization variable. $x_d^{max}$ and $x_d^{min}$ are the maximum and minimum boundaries of the variable, respectively. In this paper, our proposed algorithm is based on MFA.

Yu et al. [9] proposed a novel wise step strategy for firefly algorithm (WSSFA). In this algorithm, each firefly $X_i$ has a different adaptation step size which was defined as:

$$\alpha_i(t+1) = \alpha_i(t) - (\alpha(t) - \alpha_{min}) * e^{-\left(\left|X_{gbest}(t) - X_{i,best}(t)\right| * (t/\max\_iter)\right)}\tag{9}$$

where $t$ and max_$iter$ represents respectively represent the current number of iterations and the maximum number of iterations. The $\alpha_{min}$ is minimum step size and takes values in the interval [0, 1]. $X_{gbest}(t)$ is the best firefly individual that appears in the iterative process of algorithm evolution, and $X_{i,best}(t)$ is the solution position of the brightest firefly individual.

In 2015, Yu et al. [10] pointed out that an appropriately large step size helps the algorithm to explore the new solution space, but it is not conducive to the global convergence of the algorithm. While a relatively small step size is beneficial to the full convergence of the algorithm. Hence, they proposed a improved adaptive the step size algorithm (VSSFA), and updated the step size as follows:

$$\alpha(t) = \frac{0.4}{1 + e^{(0.015*(t-\max\_generation)/3)}}\tag{10}$$

where max_$generation$ is the maximum iteration. By testing 16 benchmark functions, the results show that VSSFA performance is greatly improved compared to FA.

Wang et al. [11] published an improved study on FA in 2016. In the improved firefly algorithm, the author proposed two simple improvement strategies: adaptive $\alpha$ strategy and dynamic $\beta$ strategy. In order to improve the convergence of the firefly optimization algorithm, the algorithm is designed to decrements the step size with the number of iterations by the following equation:

$$\alpha(t+1) = \left(1 - \frac{t}{G_{max}}\right)\alpha(t)\tag{11}$$

where it is suggested that $\alpha(0)$ should have a value of 0.5. In order to change the invariance of $\beta$ to improve the performance of the algorithm, the $\beta$ is dynamically adjusted as following:

$$\beta(t+1) = \begin{cases} rand_1, & if\ rand_2 > 0.5 \\ \beta_0(t), & else \end{cases} \tag{12}$$

Where $\beta_0(0)$ is set to 1.0. The $rand_1$ and $rand_2$ are two random numbers generated by uniform distribution. After passing the objective function experimental test, the data shows that the performance of the improved algorithm is significantly improved compared to other improved firefly algorithms.

Liu et al. [12] set the maximum and minimum values of $\alpha$ in advance, and propose a solution based on the linear drop of the maximum and minimum values of $\alpha$. The algorithm avoids the algorithm prematurely falling into the local optimum by the large interference $\alpha$ in the early stage. The step size is reduced in the later stage to improve the algorithm around the better solution and obtain better results. In the later stage, the step size is reduced to improve the algorithm around the better solution and obtain better results. Similarly, Goel and Panchal [13] also proposed a linear decrement strategy. Unlike the strategy proposed by Liu et al., the linear descending equation constructed by the algorithm has a larger magnitude.

Wang [14] proposed an $\alpha$-improvement Solution that relies only on the maximum value. The step size is inversely proportional to the square of the number of iterations, which means that it will decrease rapidly, and the random movement of fireflies almost disappears after a small number of iterations.

Yu [15] proposes an adaptive alpha, which uses the value of the best solution of the previous generation to adjust the size of the random movement parameters adaptively, effectively avoiding the premature stagnation of the algorithm. However, the mechanism of the algorithm limits the alpha to change only between (0, 1), so unless the scale factor is increased. Otherwise, the function of alpha may be too small when large area search is needed.

Another important control parameter of fireflies is the attraction step parameter $\beta$. In the firefly optimization algorithm, attraction is defined as the attraction of $\beta_0 e^{-\gamma r^2}$, and $\beta_0$ is the attraction at the light source. The attraction step parameter beta depends on the initial attraction $\beta_0$, the distance between fireflies $r$ and the light absorption coefficient $\gamma$. In recent years, the research on the parameter of attraction step size mainly focuses on the regulation of $\beta_0$ and $\gamma$. Selvarasu et al. [16] redefined the $\beta$ renewal mechanism based on the maximum $\beta\_max$ and the minimum $\beta\_min$. This renewal mechanism makes the attractive step parameter $\beta$ keep changing between $[\beta\_min, \beta\_max]$ and achieves good results. Selvarasu and Kalavathi [17] also proposed similar improvements. They limited $\beta\_max$ to (0, 1) and encoded $\beta\_min$, $\alpha$ and $\gamma$ together into the dimension of solution $x_i$, forming a self-adaptive firefly optimization algorithm with the evolution of solution, thus effectively preventing falling into local optimal solution. Gandomi et al. [18] introduced chaos theory to the firefly algorithm, and adaptively adjusted gamma and beta by twelve different chaotic graphs. The simulation results show that the effect of the chaotic optimization firefly algorithm is better than the standard firefly optimization algorithm. Jansi and AL-Wagih have done similar work. Jansi [19] and AL-Wagih [20] use Chebyshev mapping and Singusoidal mapping to adjust step parameters respectively. The experimental results show that the improved algorithm has achieved good results.

The basic principle of the above algorithm is to dynamically adjust the random step parameter or the attractive parameter with the number of iterations or the current performance state of the algorithm in different calculation modes, and increase the parameter value in the early stage of the iteration to increase the search range of the algorithm. And in the later stage, algorithms decrease the parameter value to enhance the ability of the algorithm to explore the better solution, so that the algorithm has a more complete search for the solution space. However, there is a lack of research on the knowledge and experience of the evolution of the population and the improvement and impact of their use on the location of fireflies. Although Yu et al. [21] uses the value of the best solution of the previous generation to adjust the step size random movement parameter to some extent, it limits the range of variation, making the adjustment function insufficient.

## 3  Our Proposed Firefly Algorithm

Attraction enables fireflies to move closer to the best individuals. However, in the standard firefly algorithm, our previous work found that the attraction would quickly approach 1 in the iteration process [22]. This phenomenon may make the population miss the opportunity to find the optimal solution. Figure 1, using the firefly algorithm to solve the Sphere function as an example, describes the evolution of the algorithm in the iterative process. The four triangle represents the individual of the firefly population, and the center of the circle represents the spatial location of the optimal solution. From Fig. 1, we can see that the range of the firefly population in the initial stage contains the optimal solution, but after $n$ iterations, the population shrinks and no longer contains the optimal solution.

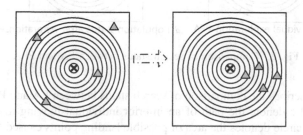

**Fig. 1.** Population status after $n$ iterations

Therefore, we consider multiplying the attraction by 0.4, so that as the algorithm iterates, the attraction portion will quickly approach 0.4 instead of 1, and $\beta$ is redefined as follow:

$$\beta(r) = 0.4 * \beta_0 e^{-\gamma r^2} \tag{13}$$

The result is that firefly individuals will tend to better individuals in a certain proportion. Meanwhile, based on the idea of proportions, we adjusted the step parameters, and $\alpha$ is redefined as follows:

$$\begin{cases} \alpha(t+1) = 0.8\alpha(t) \\ \alpha(0) = 0.4(x_d^{max} - x_d^{min}) \end{cases} \tag{14}$$

where $t$ is the current number of iterations, $x_d^{max}$ and $x_d^{min}$ represent the upper and lower bounds of the object function.

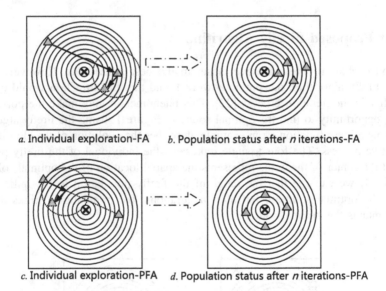

a. Individual exploration-FA      b. Population status after $n$ iterations-FA

c. Individual exploration-PFA      d. Population status after $n$ iterations-PFA

**Fig. 2.** Comparison of search status between FA and PFA

Figure 2 describes the comparison of search status between FA and PFA. The solid arrows in a and c denote the path of an inferior individual moving toward the inner ring, the dotted circle denotes the area of possible landing points caused by the moving part of the step, and the dotted triangle denotes the final position of the individual moving toward the inner ring. From the comparison of b and d in Fig. 2, we can see that after changing the attraction parameters and step size parameters, the change caused by movement can still make the group contain the global (or local) optimal solution, thus maintaining the diversity of search space.

**Table 1.** Computational results of FA based on the above analysis

| Function | Worst | Best | Mean | Std Dev |
|---|---|---|---|---|
| $f_1$ | 9.62E−111 | 5.09E−111 | **7.12E−111** | 1.01E−111 |
| $f_2$ | 4.23E−56 | 3.25E−56 | **3.67E−56** | 2.58E−57 |
| $f_3$ | 1.05E+03 | 2.14E+02 | 4.77E+02 | 2.15E+02 |
| $f_4$ | 5.28E−04 | 3.77E−56 | 2.43E−05 | 9.93E−05 |
| $f_5$ | 6.31E+02 | 2.55E+01 | 7.60E+01 | 1.23E+02 |
| $f_6$ | 1.00E+00 | 0.00E+00 | 6.67E−02 | 2.54E−01 |
| $f_7$ | 4.16E−02 | 8.04E−03 | 3.07E−02 | 1.40E−02 |
| $f_8$ | −6.71E+03 | −2.78E+03 | −4.42E+03 | 1.36E+03 |
| $f_9$ | 5.07E+01 | 1.99E+01 | 3.19E+01 | 8.92E+00 |
| $f_{10}$ | 3.24E−14 | 1.47E−14 | 2.13E−14 | 5.95E−15 |
| $f_{11}$ | 1.23E−02 | 0.00E+00 | 1.64E−03 | 3.85E−03 |
| $f_{12}$ | 1.04E−01 | 1.57E−32 | 3.47E−03 | 1.90E−02 |
| $f_{13}$ | 1.10E−02 | 3.81E−32 | 7.32E−04 | 2.79E−03 |

From Table 1, we can see that the improved firefly algorithm has better optimization effects for functions $f_1$ and $f_2$, but the results are not ideal for other functions tested. In our analysis, this phenomenon occurs because the timing of the step size reduction in the firefly algorithm does not match the objective function. Because in the previous improved firefly algorithm we set the step size to reduce the exponential model after each iteration, and this strategy is difficult to ensure that the reduced step size is adapted to the next firefly population to optimize the objective function. Of course, from the results, the step size change under this mechanism is more suitable for the functions $f_1$ and $f_2$. In order to increase the general adaptability of the firefly algorithm to different functions, we added a step change control structure based on the previous analysis to determine whether to change the step size by the movement of the best generation of the previous generation.

The PFA framework is shown in Algorithm 2. As can be seen from the PFA framework, compared with the FA algorithm framework, PFA does not increase the number of computational cycles, so PFA complexity and FA are the same.

| **Algorithm2:** Framework of PFA | |
|---|---|
| 1 | Randomly initialize $N$ fireflies (solutions) as an initial population $\{X_i | i = 1, 2, \ldots, N \}$; |
| 2 | Calculate the fitness v of each firefly $X_i$; |
| 3 | FEs = 0 and PS = $N$; |
| 4 | **while** *FEs* ≤*MAXFEs* |
| 5 | Find the best individual's ID; |
| 6 | Update the step factor $\alpha$ according to Eq. 5; |
| 7 | Update the attractiveness $\beta$ according to Eq. 9 |
| 8 | **for** *i*= 1 to *N* |
| 9 | **for** *j* = 1 to *N* |
| 10 | **if** $f(X_j) < f(X_i)$ |
| 11 | Move $X_i$ towards $X_j$ according to Eq. 4; |
| 12 | Calculate the fitness value of the new $X_i$; |
| 13 | FEs++; |
| 14 | **end if** |
| 15 | **end for** |
| 17 | **end for** |
| 18 | Calculate the brightness difference between the optimal generation of the current generation and the previous generation |
| 19 | **If** Δbrightness = 0 |
| 20 | Update the step factor $\alpha$ according to Eq. 10; |
| 21 | **end if** |
| 22 | **end while** |

## 4    Experimental Study

In this section, we have designed some numerical experiments to verify the performance of PFA. In the experiment, some benchmark functions are tested, and the simulation results of PFA are compared with other algorithms.

### 4.1    Test Problems

To verify PFA, we used 13 well-known benchmark functions [23] to test the algorithm in the following experiments. The specific function form is shown in Table 2. $f_1$–$f_5$ are unimodal functions, $f_6$ is a step function with a minimum value, and discontinuous, $f_7$ is a quadratic function with noise, and $f_8$–$f_{13}$ are multimodal functions with many local minimums.

**Table 2.** Benchmark functions used in the experiments, where $D$ is the problem dimension

| Name | Function | Search range | Global optimum |
|---|---|---|---|
| Sphere | $f_1(x) = \sum_{i=1}^{D} x_i^2$ | $[-100, 100]$ | 0 |
| Schwefel 2.22 | $f_2(x) = \sum_{i=1}^{D} |x_i| + \prod_{i=1}^{D} x_i$ | $[-10, 10]$ | 0 |
| Schwefel 1.2 | $f_3(x) = \sum_{i=1}^{D} \left(\sum_{j=1}^{i} x_j\right)^2$ | $[-100, 100]$ | 0 |
| Schwefel 2.21 | $f_4(x) = \max\{|x_i|, 1 \le i \le D\}$ | $[-100, 100]$ | 0 |
| Rosenbrock | $f_5(x) = \sum_{i=1}^{D} [100(x_{i+1} - x_i^2)^2 + (1 - x_i^2)^2]$ | $[-30, 30]$ | 0 |
| Step | $f_6(x) = \sum_{i=1}^{D} \lfloor x_i + 0.5 \rfloor$ | $[-100, 100]$ | 0 |
| Quartic with noise | $f_7(x) = \sum_{i=1}^{D} ix_i^4 + random[0, 1)$ | $[-1.28, 1.28]$ | 0 |
| Schwefel 2.26 | $f_8(x) = \sum_{i=1}^{D} -x_i \sin\left(\sqrt{|x_i|}\right) + 418.9829D$ | $[-500, 500]$ | 0 |
| Rastrigin | $f_9(x) = \sum_{i=1}^{D} [x_i^2 - 10\cos 2\pi x_i + 10]$ | $[-5.12, 5.12]$ | 0 |
| Ackley | $f_{10}(x) = -20\exp\left(-0.2\sqrt{\frac{1}{D}\sum_{i=1}^{D} x_i^2}\right)$ $-\exp\left(\frac{1}{D}\sum_{i=1}^{D} \cos(2\pi x_i)\right) + 20$ $+ e$ | $[-32, 32]$ | 0 |
| Griewank | $f_{11}(x) = \frac{1}{4000}\sum_{i=1}^{D} x_i^2 - \prod_{i=1}^{D} \cos\left(\frac{x_i}{\sqrt{i}}\right) + 1$ | $[-600, 600]$ | 0 |
| Penalized 1 | $f_{12}(x) = \frac{\pi}{D}\left\{\sum_{i=1}^{D-1} (y_i - 1)^2 [1 + \sin(\pi y_{i+1})] + (y_D - 1)^2 + 10\sin^2(\pi y_1)\right\}$ $+ \sum_{i=1}^{D} u(x_i, 10, 100, 4), y_i = 1 + (x_i + 1)/4$ $u(x_i, a, k, m) = \begin{cases} u(x_i, a, k, m), & x_i > a \\ 0, & -a \le x_i \le a \\ k(-x_i - a)^m, & x_i < -a \end{cases}$ | $[-50, 50]$ | 0 |
| Penalized 2 | $f_{13}(x) = 0.1\left\{\sin^2(3\pi x_1) + \sum_{i=1}^{D-1} (x_i - 1)^2 [1 + \sin^2(3\pi x_{i+1})] + (x_D - 1)^2 [1 + \sin^2(2\pi x_D)]\right\}$ $+ \sum_{i=1}^{D} u(x_i, 5, 100, 4)$ | $[-50, 50]$ | 0 |

## 4.2 Experimental Setup

In our experiment, PFA will be compared with the standard Firefly Optimization algorithm and three other recently proposed improved Firefly Algorithms. The design details of the parameters are shown in Table 3.

**Table 3.** The parameters of the algorithms

| | $\alpha$ | $\alpha_{min}$ | $\alpha(0)$ | $\gamma$ | $\beta$ | $\beta_{min}$ |
|---|---|---|---|---|---|---|
| FA (Yang 2010) | 0.2 | – | – | 1.0 or $1/\Gamma^2$ | $\beta_0 = 1.0$ | – |
| MFA (Fister et al. 2012) | – | – | 0.5 | $1/\Gamma^2$ | $\beta_0 = 1.0$ | 0.2 |
| WSSFA (Yu et al. 2014) | – | 0.04 | – | 1.0 | $\beta_0 = 1.0$ | – |
| VSSFA (Yu et al. 2015) | – | – | – | 1.0 | $\beta_0 = 1.0$ | – |
| PFA | Equation 10 | – | Equation 10 | $1/\Gamma^2$ | Equation 9 | – |

In order to ensure the comparability of the experimental data of each comparison algorithm, we do the same processing of its parameters, the relevant parameters are set as follows.

- Population size: 20
- Max iterations: 5.0E+05
- Run times: 30
- Problem dimension: 30

### 4.3  Comparison of Results

In Table 4, the experimental data of the 13 benchmark functions of PFA are recorded, in which "Mean" is the average result of the algorithm running 30 times and "Std Dev" is the standard deviation. From the table, it can be seen that PFA falls into the local optimal solution when optimizing the $f_5, f_8, f_9$ functions, and other objective functions have achieved good precision solutions. Especially for the $f_6$ objective function, the global optimal solution is found in each of the 30 tests.

**Table 4.** Computational results of PFA

| Function | Worst | Best | Mean | Std Dev |
|---|---|---|---|---|
| $f_1$ | 2.50E−70 | 2.75E−74 | 2.36E−71 | 4.97E−71 |
| $f_2$ | 1.58E−36 | 6.89E−39 | 1.79E−37 | 3.24E−37 |
| $f_3$ | 3.54E−15 | 2.73E−18 | 2.47E−16 | 6.55E−16 |
| $f_4$ | 9.03E−39 | 1.65E−41 | 2.53E−39 | 3.13E−39 |
| $f_5$ | 9.37E+01 | 2.11E+01 | 2.66E+01 | 1.29E+01 |
| $f_6$ | 0.00E+00 | 0.00E+00 | 0.00E+00 | 0.00E+00 |
| $f_7$ | 8.42E−02 | 1.02E−02 | 2.83E−02 | 1.46E−02 |
| $f_8$ | 6.11E+03 | 2.67E+03 | 3.78E+03 | 1.08E+03 |
| $f_9$ | 3.58E+01 | 1.29E+01 | 2.23E+01 | 6.20E+00 |
| $f_{10}$ | 4.31E−14 | 1.47E−14 | 2.50E−14 | 6.28E−15 |
| $f_{11}$ | 1.48E−02 | 0.00E+00 | 3.12E−03 | 5.01E−03 |
| $f_{12}$ | 1.04E−01 | 1.57E−32 | 3.46E−03 | 1.89E−02 |
| $f_{13}$ | 2.22E−32 | 1.57E−32 | 1.64E−32 | 1.58E−33 |

Yang proposed [6] a new version of the FA algorithm in 2010 and suggested that $\gamma = 1/\Gamma^2$, $\Gamma$ is the definition domain of the objective function. Table 5 records the experimental data comparison of two different versions of FA algorithm. As can be seen from the table, compared with the previous two versions of FA, PFA has a better performance in the test results of most functions.

In order to test the performance of PFA more comprehensively, we also compare with other improved firefly algorithms in recent years. Table 6 records the results of the data. As shown in the table, PFA performs better on functions f1, f2, f3, f4, f10, and f13 than other improved FAs.

**Table 5.** Computational results between the two versions FA and PFA

| Function | FA ($\gamma = 1.0$) | | FA ($\gamma = 1/\Gamma^2$) | | EkFA | |
|---|---|---|---|---|---|---|
| | Mean | Std dev | Mean | Std dev | Mean | Std dev |
| $f_1$ | 6.67E+04 | 1.83E+04 | 5.14E−02 | 1.36E−02 | **2.36E−71** | 4.97E−71 |
| $f_2$ | 5.19E+02 | 1.42E+02 | 1.07E+00 | 2.65E−01 | **1.79E−37** | 3.24E−37 |
| $f_3$ | 2.43E+05 | 4.85E+04 | 1.26E−01 | 1.86E−01 | **2.47E−16** | 6.55E−16 |
| $f_4$ | 8.35E+01 | 3.16E+01 | 9.98E−02 | 2.34E−02 | **2.53E−39** | 3.13E−39 |
| $f_5$ | 2.69E+08 | 6.21E+07 | 3.41E+01 | 6.23E+00 | 2.66E+01 | 1.29E+01 |
| $f_6$ | 7.69E+04 | 3.38E+03 | 5.24E+03 | 1.08E+03 | **0.00E+00** | 0.00E+00 |
| $f_7$ | 5.16E+01 | 2.46E+01 | 7.55E−02 | 1.42E−02 | **2.83E−02** | 1.46E−02 |
| $f_8$ | 1.10E+04 | 3.77E+03 | 9.16E+03 | 1.78E+03 | 3.78E+03 | 1.08E+03 |
| $f_9$ | 3.33E+02 | 6.28E+01 | 4.95E+01 | 2.39E+01 | 2.23E+01 | 6.20E+00 |
| $f_{10}$ | 2.03E+01 | 2.23E−01 | 1.21E+01 | 1.96E+00 | **2.50E−14** | 6.28E−15 |
| $f_{11}$ | 6.54E+02 | 1.69E+02 | 2.13E−02 | 1.47E−02 | **3.12E−03** | 5.01E−03 |
| $f_{12}$ | 7.16E+08 | 1.82E+08 | 6.24E+00 | 4.62E+00 | **3.46E−03** | 1.89E−02 |
| $f_{13}$ | 1.31E+09 | 4.76E+08 | 5.11E+01 | 1.28E+01 | **1.64E−32** | 1.58E−33 |

**Table 6.** Computational results of Mean best fitness value by VSSFA, WSSFA, MFA, and PFA

| Function | VSSFA Mean | WSSFA Mean | MFA Mean | PFA Mean |
|---|---|---|---|---|
| $f_1$ | 5.84E+04 | 6.34E+04 | 1.56E−05 | **2.36E−71** |
| $f_2$ | 1.13E+02 | 1.35E+02 | 1.85E−03 | **1.79E−37** |
| $f_3$ | 1.16E+05 | 1.10E+05 | 5.89E−05 | **2.47E−16** |
| $f_4$ | 8.18E+01 | 7.59E+01 | 1.73E−03 | **2.53E−39** |
| $f_5$ | 2.16E+08 | 2.29E+08 | 2.29E+01 | 2.66E+01 |
| $f_6$ | 5.48E+04 | 6.18E+04 | **0.00E+00** | **0.00E+00** |
| $f_7$ | 4.43E+01 | 3.24E−01 | 1.30E−01 | 2.83E−02 |
| $f_8$ | 1.07E+04 | 1.06E+04 | 4.84E+03 | 3.78E+03 |
| $f_9$ | 3.12E+02 | 3.61E+02 | 6.47E+01 | 2.23E+01 |
| $f_{10}$ | 2.03E+01 | 2.05E+01 | 4.23E−04 | **2.50E−14** |
| $f_{11}$ | 5.47E+02 | 6.09E+02 | 9.86E−03 | 3.12E−03 |
| $f_{12}$ | 3.99E+08 | 6.18E+08 | 5.04E−08 | 3.46E−03 |
| $f_{13}$ | 8.12E+08 | 9.13E+08 | 6.06E−07 | **1.64E−32** |

Figure 3 gives the convergence curves between FA, MFA, VSFA, WSFA and PFA. In order to increase the sensitivity of numerical differences, we make a logarithmic conversion to the fitness values of some functions (f1–f4, f7, f9–f10, f12, f13). From the Fig. 3, we can see that compared with the other four algorithms, PFA has excellent performance in convergence speed and the solution's quality on the selected benchmark functions except f7 and f12.

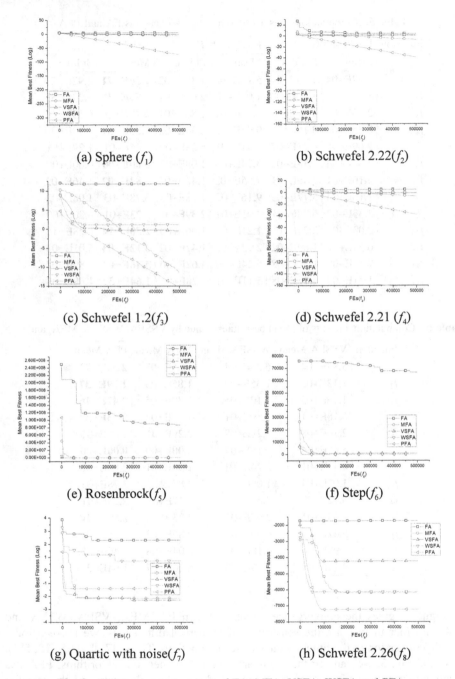

(a) Sphere ($f_1$)

(b) Schwefel 2.22($f_2$)

(c) Schwefel 1.2($f_3$)

(d) Schwefel 2.21 ($f_4$)

(e) Rosenbrock($f_5$)

(f) Step($f_6$)

(g) Quartic with noise($f_7$)

(h) Schwefel 2.26($f_8$)

**Fig. 3.** The convergence curves of FA, MFA, VSFA, WSFA and PFA

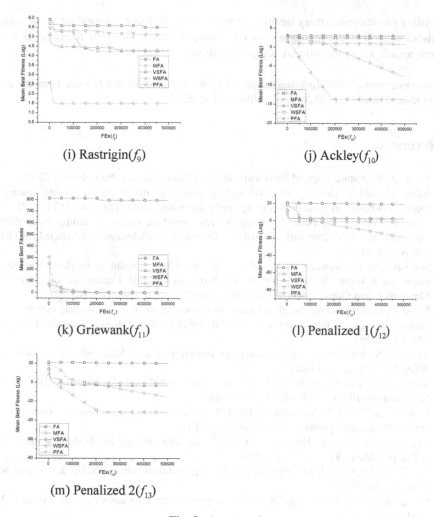

(i) Rastrigin($f_9$)

(j) Ackley($f_{10}$)

(k) Griewank($f_{11}$)

(l) Penalized 1($f_{12}$)

(m) Penalized 2($f_{13}$)

**Fig. 3.** (*continued*)

## 5 Conclusions

Based on the analysis of the attraction and step size of the firefly algorithm, a proportional firefly algorithm is proposed in this paper, with the following advantages. Firstly, the algorithm maintains the diversity of population space by attracting the whole body. Secondly, the strategy of controlling step size reduction is adapted to meet the requirement of algorithm evolution for step size change. Experimental results show that compared with other improved firefly algorithms, PFA has more advantages in solving accuracy convergence speed, and further improves the performance of the firefly algorithm.

In this paper, the proportional adjustment strategy which we proposed is mainly based on empirical data. If the proportional strategy can be adaptively adjusted according to the evolutionary iterative process, it will be more appropriate to the actual needs of algorithm optimization. For our future research, we shall focus on how to design an adaptive proportional adjustment strategy for FA.

**Acknowledgments.** This work was supported by the National Natural Science Foundation of China (No.: 61866014, 61862027, 61762040 and 61762041).

# References

1. Yang, X.-S.: Nature-Inspired Metaheuristic Algorithms. Luniver Press, Bristol (2008)
2. Jafari, O., Akbari, M.: Optimization and simulation of micrometre-scale ring resonator modulators based on p-i-n diodes using firefly algorithm. Optik **128**, 101–112 (2017)
3. Tuba, E., Mrkela, L., Tuba, M.: Support vector machine parameter tuning using firefly algorithm. In: 2016 26th International Conference Radioelektronika (RADIOELEKTRO-NIKA), pp. 413–418 (2016)
4. SundarRajan, R., Vasudevan, V., Mithya, S.: Workflow scheduling in cloud computing environment using firefly algorithm. In: 2016 International Conference on Electrical, Electronics, and Optimization Techniques (ICEEOT), pp. 955–960 (2016)
5. Shi, J.Y., et al.: Tracking the global maximum power point of a photovoltaic system under partial shading conditions using a modified firefly algorithm. J. Renew. Sustain. Energy **8**, 033501 (2016)
6. Yang, X.-S.: Engineering Optimization: An Introduction with Metaheuristic Applications. Wiley Publishing, Hoboken (2010)
7. Yang, X.-S.: Firefly algorithm, Lévy flights and global optimization, 209–218 (2010). https://doi.org/10.1007/978-1-84882-983-1_15
8. Fister Jr., I., Yang, X.-S., Fister, I., Brest, J.: Memetic firefly algorithm for combinatorial optimization. arXiv preprint arXiv:1204.5165 (2012)
9. Yu, S., Su, S., Lu, Q., Huang, L.: A novel wise step strategy for firefly algorithm. Int. J. Comput. Math. **91**, 2507–2513 (2014)
10. Yu, G.: An improved firefly algorithm based on probabilistic attraction. Int. J. Comput. Sci. Math. **7**, 530 (2016)
11. Wang, H., et al.: Firefly algorithm with adaptive control parameters. Soft. Comput. **21**, 5091–5102 (2017)
12. Liu, C., Zhao, Y., Gao, F., Liu, L.: Three-dimensional path planning method for autonomous underwater vehicle based on modified firefly algorithm. Math. Probl. Eng. **2015**, 1–10 (2015)
13. Goel, S., Panchal, V.K.: Performance evaluation of a new modified firefly algorithm. In: International Conference on Reliability, INFOCOM Technologies and Optimization, pp. 1–6 (2015)
14. Wang, G., Guo, L., Hong, D., Luo, L., Wang, H.: A modified firefly algorithm for UCAV path planning. Int. J. Hybrid Inf. Technol. **5**, 123–144 (2012)
15. Yu, S., Zhu, S., Ma, Y., Mao, D.: A variable step size firefly algorithm for numerical optimization. Appl. Math. Comput. **263**, 214–220 (2015)
16. Selvarasu, R., Kalavathi, M.S., Rajan, C.C.A.: SVC placement for voltage constrained loss minimization using self-adaptive firefly algorithm. Arch. Electr. Eng. **62**, 649–661 (2013)
17. Selvarasu, R., Kalavathi, M.S.: TCSC placement for loss minimization using self adaptive firefly algorithm. J. Eng. Sci. Technol. **10**, 291–306 (2015)

18. Gandomi, A.H., Yang, X.S., Talatahari, S., Alavi, A.H.: Firefly algorithm with chaos. Commun. Nonlinear Sci. Numer. Simul. **18**, 89–98 (2013)
19. Jansi, S., Subashini, P.: A novel fuzzy clustering based modified firefly algorithm with chaotic map for MRI brain tissue segmentation. MAGNT Res. Rep. **3**(1), 52–58 (2015)
20. Al-Wagih, K.: Improved firefly algorithm for unconstrained optimization problems. Int. J. Comput. Appl. Technol. Res. **4**, 77–81 (2014)
21. Yu, S., Yang, S., Su, S.: Self-adaptive step firefly algorithm. J. Appl. Math. **2013**, 610–614 (2013)
22. Wang, J.: Firefly algorithm with dynamic attractiveness model and its application on wireless sensor networks. Int. J. Wireless Mobile Comput. **13**, 223 (2017)
23. Lin, Y., Wang, L., Zhong, Y., Zhang, C.: Control scaling factor of cuckoo search algorithm using learning automata. Int. J. Comput. Sci. Math. **7**, 476–484 (2016)

# A Formal Taxonomy of Temporal Data Defects

João Marcelo Borovina Josko(✉)

Center of Mathematics, Computing and Cognition, Federal University of ABC,
Santo Andre, Brazil
marcelo.josko@ufabc.edu.br

**Abstract.** Data quality assessment outcomes are essential for analytical processes reliability, especially when they are related to temporal data. Such outcomes depend on efficiency and efficacy of (semi-)automated approaches that are determined by understanding the problem associated with each data defect. Despite the small number of works that describe temporal data defects regarding to accuracy, completeness and consistency, there is a significant heterogeneity of terminology, nomenclature, description depth and number of examined defects. To cover this gap, this work reports a taxonomy that organizes temporal data defects according to a five-step methodology. The proposed taxonomy enhances the descriptions and coverage of defects with regard to the related works, and also supports certain requirements of data quality assessment, including the design of visual analytics solutions to support data quality assessment.

**Keywords:** Temporal data · Data defects · Dirty data ·
Formal taxonomy · Data quality assessment · Structured data ·
Big data

## 1    Introduction

Analytical processes demand a proper data quality level to ensure reliable outcomes, specially in big data context. Improving and keeping adequate data quality level require alternatives that combine procedures, methods and techniques.

The Data Quality Assessment process (DQAp) provides practical inputs for choosing the most suitable alternative through its mapping of temporal data defects (or also temporal dirty data). To provide reliable inputs, this process requires *know about* temporal data defect structures to *know how* to assess them.

Data defects descriptions provide structural understanding of the problem associated with each defect. Such understanding is relevant for different DQAp issues, including to support the development of data quality assessment approaches [1, 4] and to establish the measurable elements of measurement-based data quality program [2, 10].

Certain literature (discussed by [5, 10]) concerned with timeless data had described very particular time-related data defects, while just one work had

© Springer Nature Switzerland AG 2019
H. Hacid et al. (Eds.): QUAT 2018, LNCS 11235, pp. 94–110, 2019.
https://doi.org/10.1007/978-3-030-19143-6_7

addressed entirely on temporal data [8]. However, the analysis of this literature shows differences in terminology, nomenclature, granularity and accuracy of description, and coverage. These restricted organization and description lead to imprecise evidence on which temporal data defects exist and their corresponding structures. Consequently, such uncertainty hampers the ability to choose the corresponding data quality assessment approach.

To address this situation, this work reports a taxonomy of temporal data defects related to *accuracy, completeness* and *consistency* quality dimensions. The taxonomy is characterized according to a five-step methodology and its main contribution is a major coverage of temporal data defects and enhanced descriptions in terms of terminology, illustrative examples and mathematical formalism. This work is organized as follows: Sect. 2 reviews all related works, while Sect. 3 presents the methodology applied to develop the proposed taxonomy and its relationship to the atemporal taxonomy by [5]. Section 4 describes the taxonomy and its basis concepts. Section 5 presents the conclusions of this work.

## 2   Related Works

This section examines works that describe defects on temporal data according to how the following questions are answered: *What is the representative set of temporal data defects related to the quality dimensions of accuracy, completeness and consistency? What is the problem structure beneath each defect?*

Certain works describe few temporal data defects, although their main subject of interest is timeless data. A previous examination of these works revealed diversity of descriptions and incomplete coverage of temporal data defects [5, 10].

In contrast, temporal data defects issues are relevant for Temporal Database [1, 14] and Statistics [15] works. These works expose the structural details of temporal data defects through some combination of textual, instance-based examples and formal resources. Nevertheless, an overall view of temporal data defects is lacked because such kind of work concentrates on very few data defects.

Lastly, taxonomies intend to provide reasonable descriptions aligned to a broad coverage and classification of data defects. A literature review determined just one taxonomy [8] concerned exclusively with temporal data defects. However, its analysis revealed uncertain descriptions and coverage. This situation is caused by the *degree of accuracy afforded by the defect definition, terminology* and *absence of theoretical support on defect selection.*

The *data defect description model* determines the degree of accuracy and clarity afforded by the defect definition. The aforementioned taxonomy uses an informal description model based on short phrases that requires interpretation and deduction effort when considered from data quality assessment perspective.

With respect to *terminology* and *nomenclature*, the taxonomy does not use terms related to temporal jargon. For instance, "Unexpected low/high values (Too long/short intervals between start-end/end-start)" is a different term applied to the same temporal data jargon of "Periodicity Constraint Violation".

The *shared absence of theoretical support* to identify the set of temporal data defects and the lack of concern with extending the descriptions contribute to an incomplete coverage of data defects. The taxonomy provides a list of temporal data defects extracted from timeless-driven works discussed at the beginning of this section. Moreover, issues regarding temporal keys, dependencies and constraints are not addressed by the taxonomy in question.

## 3    Methodological Approach to Organize the Taxonomy

The limitations and the questions discussed in Sect. 2 guided our methodology plan to follow five steps in sequence. The first step *re-examined a broad set of topics related to temporal database theory* to address issues regarding data defects coverage and to determine a proper terminology and nomenclature to be used in step five. Among the topics, but not restricted to them, it can be mentioned qualitative and quantitative temporal constraints, vacuuming and temporal dependencies [6, 7, 9, 11, 14].

These topics disclosed a broad rule set that may be applied to a relational schema to represent time-referenced facts and events of the Universe of Discourse (UoD). Each rule was basis to identify one or more violations (data defects) that lead data to defective states on the evolution of time. A subset of data defects are exclusive to temporal context (e.g., Granularity Constraint Violation) or represent structural extensions of atemporal data defects (e.g., Incorrect Reference). In contrast, some data defects have an invariant structure and show the same problem pattern independently of temporal or atemporal context. Incorrect Value, Imprecise Value, Synonymous Values and Overload Tuple are examples of such invariant defects discussed in detail by [5].

The second step *classified the temporal data defects in layers according to their shared properties*. The first layer determined whether or not such defects violate temporal rules about the UoD, named respectively as "Data Constraint" and "Fact Representation Deviation". "Data Constraint" gathers data defects that violate static or dynamic temporal rules. The former denotes explicit rules or inherent characteristics of temporal relational model (implicit rules) that states of a relation must satisfy, including participation in data relationships. In contrast, the latter comprises rules applied during state transitions of a relation. "Fact Representation Deviation" refers to defects related to differences between data representation and the corresponding fact about the objects of the UoD in one or more temporal windows. Figure 1 illustrates how identification of temporal data defect properties happened.

The third step *classified each temporal data defect based on its place or granularity of occurrence*, which are attribute value (V), single attribute (A), single tuple (T), single relation (R) or interrelation (IR), which may involve one or more database instances.

The fourth step *classified each temporal data defect according to its notion of time*. Valid time (VT) represents when a fact was true in the UoD, while transaction time (TT) refers to when a fact was known by a database. Event

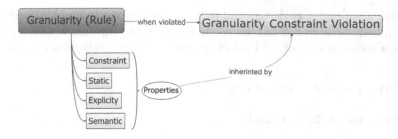

**Fig. 1.** Example of properties identification of a given temporal data defect (Source: The author)

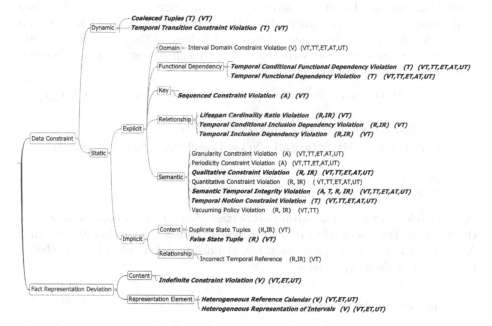

**Fig. 2.** Taxonomy of temporal data defects (Source: The author)
*Granularity:* V-Attribute Value, A-Single Attribute, T-Single Tuple, R-Single Relation, IR-Interrelations
*Temporal Notion:* VT-Valid time, TT-Transaction time, ET-Event time, AT-Availability time, UT-User Defined Time
*Note:* Data Defects in *italic* and **bold** were not addressed by any of the state-of-art taxonomies.

time (ET) is the occurrence time in the real world that generates a fact, while the availability time (AT) means the time during which the fact is believed correct. User Defined Time (UT) refers to a time for user's specific purpose.

Finally, the last step *accomplished the description of each temporal data defects* (details in Sect. 4) and it also *arranged all of them according their classifications*, as observed in Fig. 2. This figure provides an effective arrangement to identify temporal data defects and to make their properties and interrelationships explicit. Moreover, it can be combined with the timeless taxonomy [5] to provide a coherent view of data defects regarding atemporal and temporal data.

# 4  Data Defect Taxonomy

## 4.1  Structural Background

To overcome related works issues (Sect. 2) regarding descriptions accuracy and clarity, this work combined formal model, instance-based examples and short accurate texts to describe temporal data defects. The formal model uses a formalization language based on first-order temporal logic [14] that is well known by database community, as observed in Table 1. It is worth to mention that evaluating the most proper language for this goal is beyond the scope of this work. The instance-based examples were selected from a small case related to hospital domain, as shown in the logical model below.

> *Inpatient* (<u>PtID</u>, Name, BloodGroup, Address, OnsetOfSymptom, Oid, <u>PtTs</u>, PtTe)
>
> *Nurse* (<u>NuID</u>, Name, Role, Oid, <u>NrTs</u>, NrTe, NrTTs)
>
> *Treatment* (<u>TrID</u>, PtID, PtTs, NuID, NrTs, Type, Drug, Qty, Donor, #R, <u>TrTs</u>, TrTe)
>
> > PtID, PtTs references Inpatient
> > NuId, NrTs references Nurse

In this model, *Inpatient* has certain properties of ill Natural People who stay on the hospital. *Treatment* refers to the medical attention given to inpatients, while *Nurse* is who provides medical attention. An instance $I_0$ of each logical relation is observed in Tables 2, 3 and 4.

## 4.2  Taxonomy Description

Based on structural background discussed (Sect. 4.1), this section describes the higher granularity of each temporal data defect, as observed in Fig. 2. It also assumes that time is discrete, linear, bounded in the future and in the past, because this model of time is generally considered in relational databases.

**Definition 1 (Coalesced Tuples).** Let $tran : R \rightarrow R$ be a transitional function that leads the last state of $R$ to a new state $R'$, according to a inference system $R \rightarrow^{tran} R'$. Let $X$ be a subset of attributes of $R$, $X \subset R(\mathcal{D})$. Coalesced tuples occur *iff* $\exists r_i \in I(R), \exists t \in r_i(R)$ such that $t[T_s, T_e] \subset tran(t[T_s, T_e]) \wedge t[X] = tran(t[X]) \wedge t[\mathcal{O}] = tran[\mathcal{O}]$.

   Temporal coalescending is an implicitly operation that merges tuples (related to the same object) with overlapping or adjacent timestamps and explicit matching among certain attributes. However, there are organizational contexts where such operation are semantically incorrect. Coalesced tuples occur when two or more independent tuples are packed on the same tuple.

**Table 1.** Main elements of the formalization language

| | | |
|---|---|---|
| Temporal and Relational | Relational Database Schema | Set of temporal relations schemas $BD = \{R_1, ..., R_m\}$, $m \geqslant 1$ |
| | Temporal Relation Schema | Set of attributes $A = \{\mathcal{O} \cup \mathcal{D} \cup \mathcal{P}\}$ denoted by $R(A)$, $R \in DB$ |
| | Object Identity | A special attribute $\mathcal{O}$ that unequivocally identifies objects of the UoD through its lifespan in a temporal relation |
| | Data Attributes | Set of attributes $\mathcal{D} = \{a_1, ..., a_k\}$, $k \geqslant 1$. Each $a_j$, $j = [1, k]$, is regulated by a data domain $D_j$, given as $dom(a_j)$ |
| | Time-related Attributes | Set of attributes $\mathcal{P} = \{b_1, ..., b_e\}$, $e \geqslant 1$. Each $b_v$, $v = [1, e]$, is regulated by an instant or interval domain $T_t$ or $T_l$, given as $dom_{T_t}(b_v)$ or $dom_{T_l}(b_v)$, respectively |
| | Time Domain | Set of time points $\mathcal{T} = \{1, 2, ...\}$ isomorphic to the set of $\mathbb{N}$ |
| | Instant-based Domain | Discrete set of time points $\mathcal{T}$ in certain $O$ order, $T_t = (\mathcal{T}, O)$ |
| | Interval-based Domain | Set of pair $(a, b)$, given as $T_l = \{(a, b) : a \leq b, a \in \mathcal{T} \cup \{-\infty\}, b \in \mathcal{T} \cup \{+\infty\}\}$ |
| | Subset of a Relation Schema | Set of attributes $X, Y \subset R(\mathcal{D})$, where $R \in DB$ and $X \cap Y = \varnothing$ |
| | Interval Attributes | Denotes two attributes $\{T_s, T_e\}$, $T_s, T_e \subseteq R(\mathcal{P})$ and $T_s \leq T_e$, that means a period of time using closed-opened representation |
| | Temporal Relation | Finite sequence of states $I = \{r_1, ..., r_g\}$, $g \geq 1$, given as $I(R)$ |
| | State of Relation | Each state $r_f$, $f = [1, g]$, is a set of $n$ tuples $r_f = \{t_1, t_2, ..., t_n\}$ where the subscript $f$ denotes a particular time point associated with a relation denoted by $r_f(R)$ |
| | Tuple | Each tuple $t_p$, $p = [1, n]$, is a list of $q$ values $t_p = \{v_1, v_2, ..., v_q\}$ |
| | Tuple Value | Each value $v_s$, $s = [1, q]$, is a domain element of the corresponding attribute $a_s$, $b_s$ or $\mathcal{O}$, denoted as $t[a_s]$, $t[b_s]$ or $t[\mathcal{O}]$ |
| | Relationship | Referential integrity rule between relations $W$ (refer to) and $U$ (referred), denoted by $Rel : R_W \rightarrow R_U$ |
| Operators | Value Predicate Symbols | $\ominus = \{<, \leq, =, \neq, \geq, >\}$ |
| | Set Elements and Operators | $Q = \{\in, \notin, \subseteq, \subset, \cup, \cap\}$ |
| | Logical Connectives | $\{\wedge, \vee\}$ of type $Boolean \times Boolean \rightarrow Boolean$ |
| | Unary Connective | $\{\neg\}$ of type $Boolean \rightarrow Boolean$ |
| | Quantifiers | $\{\forall, \exists\}$ are the universal and existential quantifiers |
| | Operator $atnext$ | $t_i$ $atnext$ $t_j$ denotes that tuple $t_i$ exists at next time point of $t_j$ |
| | Operator $equal$ | $t_i$ $equal$ $t_j$ denotes that $t_i[T_s] = t_i[T_s]$ and $t_i[T_e] = t_i[T_e]$ |
| | Operator $overlap$ | $t_i$ $overlap$ $t_j$ is true when $T_s^i \leq T_e^j$ and $T_s^j \leq T_e^i$ |

**Table 2.** An instance of inpatient

|      | PtID | Name            | BloodGroup | Address   | OnsetOfSymptom | Oid | PtT$_s$    | PtT$_e$    |
|------|------|-----------------|------------|-----------|----------------|-----|------------|------------|
| p1:  | 1    | John Taylor     | AB−        | A Street  | Unknown        | 100 | 01/01/2018 | 02/03/2018 |
| p2:  | 1    | John Taylor     | AB+        | B Avenue  | Unknown        | 100 | 01/02/2018 | 31/12/2050 |
| p3:  | 8    | Ann P. Taylor   | AB+        | R Avenue  | 01 to 02/02/18 | 105 | 02/2018    | 03/2018    |
| p4:  | 8    | Ann P. Taylor   | AB+        | Z Street  | 28 to 28/02/18 | 105 | 03/3/2018  | 31/12/2099 |
| p5:  | 19   | Chris Taylor    | O−         | G Road    | Unknown        | 12  | 01/2/2001  | 10/09/2001 |
| p6:  | 28   | Carl de la Poll | A−         | K Avenue  | 16 to 20/9/17  | 82  | 10/12/2017 | 31/12/2099 |
| p7:  | 29   | James Bond      | A+         | T Street  | Unknown        | 86  | 01/06/2017 | 04/09/2017 |
| p8:  | 29   | James Bond      | A+         | F Street  | 05/09/17       | 86  | 05/09/2017 | 31/12/2099 |
| p9:  | 41   | John P. Jones   | A−         | R Avenue  | 07 to 09/04/18 | 201 | 02/05/2018 | 31/12/2099 |
| p10: | 53   | John Paul Jones | A          | R Square  | 09/10/18       | 409 | 10/10/2018 | 31/12/2099 |
| p11: | 58   | Billy Plant     | AB+        | F Street  | Unknown        | 130 | 02/03/2018 | 25/07/2018 |
| p12: | 58   | Billy Plant     | AB+        | K Road    | 25/07/18       | 130 | 25/07/2018 | 13/03/2018 |

**Table 3.** An instance of nurse

|      | NuID | Name          | Role      | Oid | NrTs       | NrTe       | NrTTs      |
|------|------|---------------|-----------|-----|------------|------------|------------|
| nu1: | 6    | Vika Farm     | Head II   | 109 | 01/01/2001 | 31/12/2006 | 04/01/2001 |
| nu2: | 4    | Joane Rhodes  | Level I   | 491 | 10/12/2008 | 31/12/2009 | 15/12/2016 |
| nu3: | 6    | Vika Farm     | Level V   | 109 | 01/01/2007 | 31/12/2017 | 02/01/2018 |
| nu4: | 8    | Susan Knotz   | Level I   | 612 | 20/01/2015 | 19/02/2018 | 20/01/2015 |
| nu5: | 4    | Joane Rhodes  | Level II  | 491 | 01/01/2010 | 28/02/2018 | 04/01/2010 |
| nu6: | 6    | Vika Farm     | Head I    | 109 | 01/01/2018 | 31/12/2099 | 02/01/2018 |
| nu7: | 4    | Joane Rhodes  | Level III | 491 | 01/03/2018 | 31/12/2099 | 04/01/2018 |
| nu8: | 8    | Susan Knotz   | Level II  | 612 | 20/02/2018 | 31/12/2099 | 20/01/2018 |

**Table 4.** An instance of treatment

|       | TrID | PtID | PtT$_s$    | NuID | NrTs       | Type | Drug | Qty  | Donor | #R | TrT$_s$    | TrT$_e$    |
|-------|------|------|------------|------|------------|------|------|------|-------|----|------------|------------|
| tr1:  | 12   | 28   | 10/12/2017 | 4    | 01/01/2010 | X1   | EPC  | 2.00 |       | 3  | 11/12/2017 | 15/12/2017 |
| tr2:  | 13   | 28   | 10/12/2017 | 4    | 01/01/2010 | BTr  | -    | -    |       | 3  | 16/12/2017 | 20/12/2017 |
| tr3:  | 18   | 41   | 02/05/2018 | 6    | 01/01/2018 | FB   | FYC  | 1.80 |       | 4  | 29/04/2018 | 30/05/2018 |
| tr4:  | 33   | 19   | 01/02/2001 | 6    | 01/01/2001 | BTr  | -    | -    | Anna  | 5  | 04/01/2001 | 10/01/2001 |
| tr5:  | 88   | 8    | 03/03/2018 | 6    | 01/01/2018 | A    | HAL  | 20.0 |       | 8  | 03/03/2018 | 05/03/2018 |
| tr6:  | 90   | 8    | 03/03/2018 | 4    | 01/03/2018 | A    | T5A  | 3.20 |       | 8  | 06/03/2018 | 10/03/2018 |
| tr7:  | 92   | 8    | 03/03/2018 | 8    | 20/02/2018 | A    | HAL  | 22.0 |       | 8  | 11/03/2018 | 29/03/2018 |
| tr8:  | 93   | 58   | 02/03/2018 | 8    | 20/02/2018 | Exm  | -    | -    |       | 8  | 02/03/2018 | 06/03/2018 |
| tr9:  | 95   | 58   | 02/03/2018 | 4    | 01/03/2018 | CH   | NoX  | 1.8  |       | 8  | 11/03/2018 | 12/03/2018 |
| tr10: | 96   | 1    | 01/02/2018 | 8    | 20/02/2018 | A    | HAL  | 19.5 |       | 3  | 01/02/2018 | 07/02/2018 |
| tr11: | 98   | 1    | 01/02/2018 | 4    | 01/01/2010 | A    | T5A  | 5.5  |       | 3  | 08/02/2018 | 13/02/2018 |
| tr12: | 99   | 1    | 01/02/2018 | 8    | 20/01/2015 | A    | T5A  | 7.0  |       | 3  | 16/02/2018 | 17/02/2018 |
| tr13: | 109  | 58   | 25/07/2018 | 6    | 01/01/2018 | CH   | NoX  | 2.0  |       | 5  | 25/07/2018 | 25/07/2018 |

*Example:* The tuple $tr1$ is the result of a coalescing operation between two adjacent tuples related to a continuous treatment.

**Definition 2 (Duplicate State Tuples).** Let $X_1$ and $X_2$ be attribute subsets, where $X_1 \subset R_1(\mathcal{D})$ and $X_2 \subset R_2(\mathcal{D})$. Let $X_1$ and $X_2$ be pairwise compatible, where for all $a_1^i \in X_1$ and $a_2^i \in X_2$, $i \in [1, k]$, $k \geq 1$, $dom(a_1^i)$ and $dom(a_2^i)$ are identical. Let $\simeq_i$ be the record matching similarity predicate on attributes $a_1^1 \simeq_1 a_2^1 \wedge ... \wedge a_1^k \simeq_k a_2^k$, denote as $X_1 \simeq X_2$. There are duplicate state tuples *iff* $\exists r_i \in I(R_1), \exists r_j \in I(R_2), \exists t_1 \in r_i(R_1), \exists t_2 \in r_j(R_2)$ such that $t_1[X_1] \simeq t_2[X_2] \wedge (t_1 \ overlap \ t_2 \vee t_1 \ equal \ t_2)$.

This defect denotes multiple states tuples from one or more relations that refer to the same object in the UoD. Their data attributes may have identical values, certain similarity degree or be mostly divergent. Moreover, their time-related attributes may have equal or overlapped timestamps.

*Example:* The overlapped tuples $p9$ and $p10$ represent the same inpatient in the UoD with similar values in almost all the attributes.

**Definition 3 (False State Tuple).** Let $fstup : r(R) \rightarrow \{true, false\}$ be a function which returns if a state tuple from $R$ complies with the rules that define its usefulness for the UoD. A state tuple is false *iff* $\exists r_i \in I(R), \exists t \in r_i(R)$ such that $ftsup(t)$ is *false*.

A temporal database must represent only the real changes on objects over time. A state tuple is false when it represents an inexistent object change in real world.

*Example:* The tuple $p4$ represent a change on inpatient address that have never happened.

**Definition 4 (Granularity Constraint Violation).** Let $\mathcal{G}_\mathcal{R}$ be the granularity defined for temporal attributes $\mathcal{P}$ of relation $R$. Let $grain : r(R) \rightarrow \{true, false\}$ be a function which returns if a value of a time-related attribute complies with the granularity $\mathcal{G}_\mathcal{R}$. This defect occurs *iff* $\exists r_i \in I(R), \exists t \in r_i(R), \exists a \in R(\mathcal{P})$ such that $grain(t[a])$ is *false*.

Granularity specifies the temporal qualification of time-related attributes, including general (e.g, hour, day) or context-oriented (e.g., business day, academic semester) qualifiers. There is a granularity constraint violation when a value of a given time-related attribute does not match the permissible granularity.

*Example:* The Inpatient tuple $p3$ uses *month* as temporal qualification, although such relation requires *day* as granularity.

**Definition 5 (Heterogeneous Reference Calendar).** Let $\mathcal{C}_\mathcal{L}$ be a set of reference calendars. Let $refCal : r(R) \rightarrow \mathcal{C}_\mathcal{L}$ be a function that returns the reference calendar associated to a time-related attribute $a$ of relation $R$, $a \in R(\mathcal{P})$. A heterogeneous calendar occurs *iff* $\exists r_i \in I(R), \exists t_1 \in r_i(R), \forall t_2 \in r_i(R), t_1 \neq t_2$ such that $refCal(t_1) \neq refCal(t_2)$.

A calendar ascribes a meaning to temporal values that is basis for human interpretation. Organizations may use different reference calendars to run its business, including financial and fiscal. A heterogeneous situation occurs when a time-related attribute represents timestamps with two or more calendars.

*Example:* The treatment $tr1$ uses accounting calendar (when the treatment cost was accounted) instead of the hospital working days calendar (when the treatment really started).

**Definition 6 (Heterogeneous Representation of Intervals).** Let $\mathcal{I}_\mathcal{N}$ be an interval representation defined to interval attributes of relation $R$. Let $het$ : $r(R) \times r(R) \longrightarrow \{true, false\}$ be a function that returns if states tuples of $R$ comply with $\mathcal{I}_\mathcal{N}$. A heterogeneous representation occurs *iff* $\exists r_i, r_j \in I(R), \exists t_1 \in r_i(R), \exists t_2 \in r_j(R)$ such that $t_1[\mathcal{O}] = t_2[\mathcal{O}] \wedge t_2$ *atnext* $t_1 \wedge het(t_1, t_2)$ is *false*.

An interval denotes an amount of the time delimited by two time-related attributes, named *start* $(T_s)$ and *end* $(T_e)$. There are four variants of interval representation (closed-opened, closed-closed, opened-closed, opened-opened) that differ on how start and end attributes are interpreted along the time line: inclusive or not. This defect occurs when certain timestamps of an interval attribute represent facts about objects of the UoD using different representations.

*Example:* The Inpatient tuples $p7$ and $p8$ use different representation of intervals (closed-opened and closed-closed, respectively), while the required one is closed-opened. Such situation leads to an interpretation gap.

**Definition 7 (Incorrect Temporal Reference).** Let $Rel : R_1 \to R_2$ be a relationship set between temporal relations $R_1, R_2$. Incorrect temporal reference occurs *iff* $\exists (t_i, t_j) \in Rel$ such that $t_i[T_s, T_e] \not\subseteq t_j[T_s, T_e]$.

This occasion refers to a relationship instance that valid time of *refer to* relation is not included in valid time of *referred* relation, although it obeys all of the other rules.

*Example:* The timestamp of treatment $tr3$ does not match with the timestamp of referred inpatient $p9$.

**Definition 8 (Indefinite Constraint Violation).** Let $I^{T_s}$ be a constraint defined for $T_s$ that regulates the period of time from $p_1$ to $p_2$ during which a fact or event may be true, $p_1 \leq T_s \leq p_2$. Let $I^{T_e}$ be a analogue constraint for $T_e$. Let $checkIC : r(R) \to \{true, false\}$ be a function which returns if time-related attributes of a tuple of $R$ comply with indefinite constraints $I^{T_s}, I^{T_e}$. The indefinite constraint violation occurs *iff* $\exists r_i \in I(R), \exists t \in r_i(R)$ such that $checkIC(t[T_s, T_e])$ is *false*.

Temporal indeterminacy refers to events or facts whose corresponding associated time is uncertain. Such uncertainty can be expressed by a conjunction of constraints based on interval relationships. Time-related attributes of one or more tuples that do not comply with such constraints constitutes a violation.

*Example:* To a proper treatment, declaration of the onset of symptoms must have a precision of around three days. However, the inpatient $p6$ violate such constraint.

**Definition 9 (Interval Domain Constraint Violation).** The domain violation occurs *iff* $\exists r_i \in I(R), \exists t \in r_i(R)$ such that $t[T_s, T_e] \notin dom_{Tl}(T_s, T_e)$.

This constraint regulates the allowed values for the two forming attributes of an interval. In this work, an interval domain constraint refers to a maximum or minimal duration of time, interval ending point, timezones parity and start-end attributes relationship (e.g., $\leq$). Violation arises when a pair of timestamps does not comply with the permissible domain of the interval attribute.

*Example:* The tuple $p2$ uses $31/12/2050$ instead of $31/12/2099$ as interval ending point.

**Definition 10 (Lifespan Cardinality Ratio Violation).** Let $lcr : R_1 \times R_2 \to \mathbb{N}$ be a function that maps the lifespan cardinality ratio of $Rel : R_1 \to R_2$. Let $s : r(R_1) \times r(R_2) \to \mathbb{N}$ be a function defined as follows: $s(a,b)$ is 1 if $a = b$ or 0 if otherwise. The cardinality violation occurs *iff* $\forall r_i \in I(R_1), \forall r_j \in I(R_2), \exists t_1 \in r_i(R_1), \exists t_2 \in r_j(R_2)$ such that $\sum s(t_1[W], t_2[U]) > lcr(R_1, R_2)$.

The lifespan cardinality ratio establishes the maximum number of relationship instances so that each object from a relation can participate within a binary relationship during its lifespan. A violation occurs when any object does not comply with the maximum as the *referred* or *refer to* role.

*Example:* The hospital is authorized to administer treatment "CH" just once for any inpatient. Nevertheless, a given inpatient received such treatment twice ($tr9$ and $tr13$).

**Definition 11 (Periodicity Constraint Violation).** Let $\mathcal{R}_P$ be a expression that defines a non-overlapping and non-meeting repeating pattern of time instants with period $p$ and granularity $g$ defined for $R$. Let *periodic* $: r(R) \to \{true, false\}$ be a function which returns if state tuples of $R$ comply with the repeating pattern defined by $\mathcal{R}_P$. The periodicity violation occurs *iff* $\exists r_i, r_j \in I(R), \exists t_1 \in r_i(R), \exists t_2 \in r_j(R)$ such that $t_2$ *atnext* $t_1 \wedge t_1[\mathcal{O}] = t_2[\mathcal{O}] \wedge periodic(t_1, t_2)$ is *false*.

Periodicity denotes phenomena (e.g., events) that have a pattern of repetition in time. Such pattern may be strongly periodic (equally distant moments in time), nearly periodic (regular phenomena but not equally distant moments in time) and intermittent. A periodicity constraint violation arises when certain phenomenon (represented by a tuple) about a given object of the UoD does not match the required repeating pattern for a temporal relation.

*Example:* For all inpatients, one treatment immediately succeeds the other. However, there is an inpatient $p1$ whose treatments have a gap ($tr11, tr12$).

**Definition 12 (Qualitative Constraint Violation).** Let $\mathcal{Q_L}$ be a set of temporal relationships defined for the interval attributes $T_s, T_e$ of relation $R$, given as $\mathcal{Q_L} = \{qual_1, ..., qual_z\}$, $z \geqslant 1$. Let $match : r(R) \times r(R) \times \mathcal{Q_L} \to \{true, false\}$ be a function that returns if states tuples of $R$ comply with a certain temporal relationship of $\mathcal{Q_L}$. There is a qualitative constraint violation *iff* $\exists r_i \in I(R), \exists t_1, t_2 \in r_i(R), t_1 \neq t_2, \exists qual \in \mathcal{Q_L}$ such that $match(t_1, t_2, qual)$ is *false*.

A qualitative constraint establishes a temporal relationship among facts about the objects of the UoD. Such relationships consider several operators (e.g., set, comparison, interval algebra) to express relationships between time-related attributes. A violation arises when one of these relationships is disobeyed.

*Example:* Any blood transfusion (treatment type "BTr") must be preceded by a medical exam. However, such rule was not followed by treatments $tr2$ and $tr4$.

**Definition 13 (Quantitative Constraint Violation).** Let $\mathcal{Q_T}$ be the set of permissible interval values defined for the time-related attribute $a$ of relation $R$, $a \in R(\mathcal{P})$, given as $\mathcal{Q_T} = \{[m_1, n_1], ..., [m_z, n_z]\}$, $m_h \neq n_h, 1 < h \leq k, k \geq 1$. Let $match : r(R) \times r(R) \times \mathcal{Q_T} \longrightarrow \{true, false\}$ be a function which returns if the distance between state tuples of $R$ comply with a certain permissible interval of $\mathcal{Q_T}$. There is a quantitative constraint violation *iff* $\exists r_i, r_j \in I(R), \exists t_1 \in r_i(R), \exists t_2 \in r_j(R), \forall [m_3, n_3] \in \mathcal{Q_T}$ such that $match(t_1[a], t_2[a], [m_3, n_3])$ is *false*.

A quantitative constraint refers to the absolute location or distance between time instants of facts about objects of the UoD. Such issues is usually determined by a set of permissible interval values. A quantitative violation arises when the location or distance between two or more tuples disobey the permissible set.

*Example:* Inpatients that perform a medical exam (treatment type "Exm") must be followed within 24 hours by a treatment session. However, the treatments $tr8$ and $tr9$ disobeyed such constraint.

**Definition 14 (Sequence Constraint Violation).** Let $X$ be an attribute subset of $R$, $X = Y \cup T_s$, $Y \subseteq R(\mathcal{D})$. Let $M$ be an attribute subset of $R$, $M \cap X = \varnothing$. Let $R(A)$ be key dependent on $X$ such that $X \to R(A)$. This constraint is violated *iff* $\exists r_i, r_j \in I(R), \exists t_1 \in r_i(R), \exists t_2 \in r_j(R), \exists a \in R(\mathcal{D})$ such that $t_1[\mathcal{O}] = t_2[\mathcal{O}] \wedge t_1[Y] = t_2[Y] \wedge t_2$ *atnext* $t_1 \wedge ((t_1[a] \neq t_2[a] \wedge t_1$ *overlap* $t_2) \vee (t_1[T_e] = t_2[T_s] + 1 \wedge t_1[M] = t_2[M]) \vee (t_1[M] = t_2[M] \wedge t_1$ *overlap* $t_2))$.

The purpose of the temporal key is guarantee that no object can have contradictory states at the same time or repeated states at same or adjacent time. Violations may have two origins: *i*) two or more tuples with overlapping timestamps share different values for certain data attributes, *ii*) two or more tuples with overlapping or adjacent timestamps share the same value for their data attributes.

*Example:* The overlapped tuples $p1$ and $p2$ refers to the same object in a contradictory way.

**Definition 15 (Semantic Temporal Integrity Violation).** Let $Rel : R_1 \to R_2$ be a relationship set between temporal relations $R_1$ and $R_2$. Let $\mathcal{S}_\mathcal{R}$ be the set of semantic rules on relationship $Rel$, denoted as $\mathcal{S}_\mathcal{R} = \{rule_1, ..., rule_z\}$, $z \geqslant 1$. Let $match : Rel \times \mathcal{S}_\mathcal{R} \to \{true, false\}$ be a function which returns if an instance of relationship $Rel$ complies with a certain semantic rule of $\mathcal{S}_\mathcal{R}$. There is a violation iff $\exists(t_1, t_2) \in Rel, \exists rule \in \mathcal{S}_\mathcal{R}$ such that $match(t_1, t_2, rule)$ is $false$.

The semantic temporal integrity comprises a set of complex rules for an UoD that guarantees consistency on data changed over time. For instance, theses rules may consist of n-ary qualitative-quantitative constraints or refers to any number of states of a relation (e.g, salary value must be progressive on time). A violation arises when one of these rules is disobeyed.

*Example:* The drugs "HAL" and "T5A" must be given to inpatients for 4 and 2 days, respectively, in two cycles. However, this medical treatment constraint is ignored in case of inpatient $p1$ ($tr10$ to $tr12$).

**Definition 16 (Temporal Conditional Functional Dependency Violation).** Let $Tp$ be a pattern tableau with attributes in $X_p$, $Y_p$ and $Z_p^T$, where for each pattern tuple $tp \in Tp$, $tp[a]$, $a \in X_p \cup Y_p$, is either a particular value in dom(a) or a "wildcard" symbol "_" that draws values from dom(a), and $tp[b]$, $b \in Z_p^T$, is a particular value in $dom_{T_i}(b)$ or a "wildcard" symbol "_" that draws values from $dom_{T_i}(b)$. Let $Y_p$ be conditionally dependent on $X_p$ and $Z_p^T$ defined as $(X_p, Z_p^T \to Y_p, Tp)$ on relation $R$. This conditional dependency is violated iff $\exists r_i \in I(R), \exists t_1, t_2 \in r_i(R), t_1 \neq t_2$, such that $t_1[X_p] = t_2[X_p] = tp[X_p] \wedge (t_1[Y_p] = t_2[Y_p] \neq tp[Y_p] \vee t_1[Y_p] \neq t_2[Y_p] \vee t_1[Z_p] = t_2[Z_p] \neq tp[Z_p] \vee t_1[Z_p] \neq t_2[Z_p])$.

A conditional functional dependency $(A \to B, Tp)$ on a relation $R$ denotes that $B$ values depend functionally on $A$ values only for the tuples of $R$ that satisfies a temporal data pattern specified at $Tp$. Such pattern may be based on an instant or interval domain. A violation arises when this constraint is not obeyed by a some $B$ value.

*Example:* The Treatment relation has a conditional functional dependency between Type, TrTs and Donor, denoted by $[Type, TrTs \to Donor, Tp]$. Pattern Tableau $Tp$ specifies that treatment type "BTr" (Blood Transfusion) for the months of "December" and "January" must have the main (blood) donor name. However, the tuple $tr2$ violates this pattern.

**Definition 17 (Temporal Conditional Inclusion Dependency Violation).** Let $Rel : R_1 \to R_2$ be a relationship set between temporal relations $R_1$ and $R_2$. Let $exp : Rel \to \mathbb{N}$ be a function that apply a temporal relationship or expression on instances of $Rel$. Let $Tp$ be a pattern tableau with attributes in $X_p$, $Y_p$, $X_p^T$ and $Y_p^T$, where for each attribute $a \in X_p \cup Y_p$ and $b \in X_p^T \cup Y_p^T$, and for each tuple $tp \in Tp$, $tp[a]$ is a value in $dom(a)$ and $tp[b]$ is a value in $dom_{T_i}(b)$. Let $R_1$ be conditionally dependent in time on $R_2$, as represented by $(R_1[X; X_p, X_p^T] \subseteq R_2[Y; Y_p, Y_p^T], Tp)$. This dependency is violated *iff* $\exists (t_1, t_2) \in Rel$ such that $t_1[X_p] = tp[X_p] \wedge t_2[Y_p] = tp[Y_p] \wedge exp(t_1[X_p^T],$ $t_2[Y_p^T]) \neq exp(tp[X_p^T], tp[Y_p^T])$.

To ensure referential integrity consistency, certain relationships must obey temporal conditions. A violation arises when there is a relationship instance that do not follow some of these conditions.

*Example:* The treatment type "FB" is not allowed when the difference between onset of symptom and the beginning of treatment is superior than one week. However, there is an inpatient treatment $tr3$ that violates such condition.

**Definition 18 (Temporal Functional Dependency Violation).** Let $\xi$ be an expression used to select tuples at different time points. Let $\Gamma$ be a time relation defined on a pair of time points $(i, j)$ such that $i, j \in \mathcal{T}$. Let $Y$ be functionally dependent on $X$, denoted by $X \rightarrow_{\xi, \Gamma} Y$, $X, Y \subseteq R(\mathcal{D})$. This dependency is violated *iff* $\exists r_i, r_j \in I(R), \exists t_1 \in r_i(R), \exists t_2 \in r_j(R), t_1[\mathcal{O}] = t_2[\mathcal{O}]$, such that $t_1[X] = t_2[X]$ and $t_1[Y] \neq t_2[Y]$.

A temporal functional dependency $(A \rightarrow_{\xi, \Gamma} B)$ denotes that each $B$ values is associated with precisely one $A$ value for a set of tuples defined by expression $\xi$ and according to a time relation or a granularity set $\Gamma$. A violation arises when this constraint is not obeyed by some $B$ value.

*Example:* During an inpatient treatment, the quantity of the second administration depends on the first quantity administrated. Even so, there are two treatments $(tr11 - tr12$ and $tr5 - tr7)$ that defy such regulation.

**Definition 19 (Temporal Inclusion Dependency Violation).** Let $Rel :$ $R_1 \rightarrow R_2$ be a relationship set between temporal relations $R_1, R_2$. There is an temporal inclusion dependency violation *iff* $\exists r_i \in I(R_1), \forall r_j \in I(R_2), \exists t_1 \in r_i(R_1), \forall t_2 \in r_j(R_2)$ such that $t_1[W] \neq t_2[U] \vee t_1[T_s, T_e] \not\subseteq t_2[T_s, T_e]$.

Temporal inclusion dependency imposes temporal acceptance rules on actions over instances of relationships to ensure referential integrity consistency. A violation is created when a tuple $t_1$ refers to tuple $t_2$ that is available for the referred relation, but they share incompatible timestamps.

*Example:* The treatment $tr4$ had started long before the inpatient $p5$ was hospitalized.

**Definition 20 (Temporal Notion Constraint Violation).** Let $N_1, N_2$ be two sets of time-related attribute with different semantic, $N_1, N_2 \subset R(\mathcal{P})$. Let $\mathcal{N}_C$ be the set of relationship rules among $N_1, N_2$, denoted as $\mathcal{N}_C = \{rule_1, ..., rule_q\}$, $q \geqslant 1$. Let $match : r(R) \times \mathcal{N}_C \rightarrow \{true, false\}$ be a function which returns if a state tuple of $R$ complies with a certain rule of $\mathcal{N}_C$. There is a violation *iff* $\exists r_i \in I(R), \exists t \in r_i(R), \exists rule \in \mathcal{N}_C$ such that $match(t[N_1, N_2], rule)$ is *false*.

Temporal notion ascribes a semantic meaning to time-related attributes, including valid time, transaction time and event time. Combining different notions of time implies that certain relationship rules (according to UoD) among each other must be follow. Ignoring one of such rules leads to a violation.

*Example:* All nurses records must be kept in sync to their roles (responsibilities) along time. However, certain nurses records ($nu2$ and $nu3$) refer to retroactive actions as its transaction time (NrTTS) is greater than valid end time (NrTe).

**Definition 21 (Temporal Transition Constraint Violation).** Let $\xi$ be an expression used to select tuples at different time points regarding a particular object $\mathcal{O}$. Let $\mathcal{T_T}$ be the set of transition rules of object $\mathcal{O}$, denoted as $\mathcal{T_T} = \{rule_1, ..., rule_q\}$, $q \geqslant 1$. Let $comply : r(R) \times \mathcal{T_T} \rightarrow_{\xi} \{true, false\}$ be a function which returns if an object of $R$ complies with all $\mathcal{T_T}$ transition rules. A transition violation occurs *iff* $\exists r_i, r_j \in I(R), \exists t_i \in r_i(R), \exists t_j \in r_j(R)$ such that $t_i[\mathcal{O}] = t_j[\mathcal{O}] \wedge t_j$ *atnext* $t_i \wedge comply(t_i)$ is true $\wedge$ $comply(t_j)$ is false.

Temporal transition is a dynamic constraint that gathers rules that ensure the valid state transition of an object of UoD based on its past states (i.e., history). Such rules are evaluated when a given object attempts to evolves and changes its role (e.g., become a new specialization on a generalization structure). Successive disjunctions roles, repeatable roles according previous role pattern, transition to a new object according previous states of a base object are examples of temporal transition rules. A violation refers to an object whose evolution did not obey one of these dynamic rules.

*Example:* In accordance with hospital human resources policy, nurses must follow a set of successive and progressive roles. However, nurses records $nu1$, $nu3$ and $nu6$ violate such rule.

**Definition 22 (Vacuuming Policy Violation).** Let $V$, $V \subset \mathcal{T}$, be the vacuuming policy criteria defined for temporal relation $R$. A vacuuming violation occurs *iff* $\exists r_i \in I(R)$ such that $i \notin V$.

Temporal databases should provide a complete record of the past. However, part of the past is not demanded because of business requirements or data management complexity. Vacuuming policy defines data expiration criteria (time range or maximum number of states) usually relative to the current time. A violation occurs when any state of a relation does not comply with the vacuuming criteria.

*Example:* The hospital policy determines to keep the last 15 years of inpatients records counting from the current year. However, tuple $p5$ disobey such policy.

## 4.3   Connection with Quality Dimensions

Quality dimensions embody all assessment perspectives of data or information, highlighting the DQAp multidimensional nature. Literature provides somewhat heterogeneous dimension definitions discussed by certain works that attempt to establish a basis for consensus building [12].

Regardless of definition variations, most of the literature classify quality dimensions based on *the target object* and *the target aspect*. The first refers to the object of assessment, which are data or information. The latter defines what object aspect is assessed which comprises of content, structure and metadata, use context or process of availability. *Accuracy, completeness* and *consistency* (this work's focus) are quality dimensions related to data and content perspectives.

In this work, accuracy is the fidelity level between a certain database value and its corresponding value in the real world or reference basis. Consistency refers to violation of rules and constraints applied to data to ensure UoD needs. Finally, completeness is the expected comprehensiveness of data in a database in regard to the corresponding facts of the UoD. These definitions were based on literature [12, 13] and it is beyond the scope of this work to provide a consensus definitions. Table 5 shows the association between the aforementioned quality dimensions and the taxonomy's data defects. Such arrange is similar to timeless data defects by [3].

**Table 5.** Association between quality dimensions and temporal defects

| Quality dimension | Temporal data defect |
|---|---|
| Accuracy | Coalesced Tuples |
| | Duplicate State Tuples |
| | Granularity Constraint Violation |
| | Heterogeneous Reference Calendar |
| | Heterogeneous Representation of Intervals |
| | Incorrect Temporal Reference |
| Completeness | False State Tuple |
| Consistency | Indefinite Constraint Violation |
| | Interval Domain Constraint Violation |
| | Lifespan Cardinality Ratio Violation |
| | Periodicity Constraint Violation |
| | Qualitative Constraint Violation |
| | Quantitative Constraint Violation |
| | Sequence Constraint Violation |
| | Semantic Temporal Integrity Violation |
| | Temporal Conditional Functional Dependency Violation |
| | Temporal Conditional Inclusion Dependency Violation |
| | Temporal Functional Dependency Violation |
| | Temporal Inclusion Dependency Violation |
| | Temporal Notion Constraint Violation |
| | Temporal Transition Constraint Violation |
| | Vacuuming Policy Violation |

# 5  Conclusions

This work reports a taxonomy that organized a detailed description of temporal data defects regarding to the quality dimensions of accuracy, completeness and consistency. The taxonomy applied a five-step methodology to address all the issues discussed in Sect. 2: the theoretical review enabled the systematic and broad coverage of temporal data defects (fifteen defects were not addressed by the state-of-art taxonomies, as highlighted in Fig. 2), and improved the data defect descriptions; the classification steps organized data defects according to their properties, granularity of occurrence and notion of time.

The taxonomy structure can support relevant issues in temporal data quality assessment, including the training of data quality appraisers and parameter setting of (un)supervised data defect detections approaches. Nevertheless, the taxonomy does not address spatial data as well as it offers high level formal descriptions of some defects that involve complex and broad rules. In future works, this taxonomy will be the basis for designing a semi-supervised visual approach for temporal data quality assessment.

# References

1. Abedjan, Z., Akcora, C.G., Ouzzani, M., Papotti, P., Stonebraker, M.: Temporal rules discovery for web data cleaning. Proc. VLDB Endowment 9(4), 336–347 (2015)
2. Berti-Equille, L., et al.: Assessment and analysis of information quality: a multidimensional model and case studies. Int. J. Inf. Qual. 2(4), 300–323 (2011)
3. Borovina Josko, J.M.: Uso de propriedades visuais-interativas na avaliação da qualidade de dados. Doctoral dissertation, Universidade de São Paulo (2016)
4. Borovina Josko, J.M., Ferreira, J.E.: Visualization properties for data quality visual assessment: an exploratory case study. Inf. Vis. 16(2), 93–112 (2017)
5. Josko, J.M.B., Oikawa, M.K., Ferreira, J.E.: A formal taxonomy to improve data defect description. In: Gao, H., Kim, J., Sakurai, Y. (eds.) DASFAA 2016. LNCS, vol. 9645, pp. 307–320. Springer, Cham (2016). https://doi.org/10.1007/978-3-319-32055-7_25
6. Chomicki, J., Toman, D.: Time in database systems. Handbook of Temporal Reasoning in Artificial Intelligence. 1, 429–467 (2005)
7. Combi, C., Montanari, A., Sala, P.: A uniform framework for temporal functional dependencies with multiple granularities. In: Pfoser, D. et al. (eds.) International Symposium on Spatial and Temporal Databases. SSTD 2011. LNCS, vol. 6849, pp. 404–421. Springer, Heidelberg (2011). https://doi.org/10.1007/978-3-642-22922-0_24
8. Gschwandtner, T., Gärtner, J., Aigner, W., Miksch, S.: A taxonomy of dirty time-oriented data. In: Quirchmayr, G., Basl, J., You, I., Xu, L., Weippl, E. (eds.) CD-ARES 2012. LNCS, vol. 7465, pp. 58–72. Springer, Heidelberg (2012). https://doi.org/10.1007/978-3-642-32498-7_5
9. Jensen, C.S., Snodgrass, R.T.: Temporal specialization and generalization. IEEE Trans. Knowl. Data Eng. 6(6), 954–974 (1994)

10. Laranjeiro, N., Soydemir, S.N., Bernardino, J.: A survey on data quality: classifying poor data. In: 21st Pacific Rim International Symposium on Dependable Computing, pp. 179–188. IEEE Press, Zhangjiajie (2015)
11. Meiri, I.: Combining qualitative and quantitative constraints in temporal reasoning. Artif. Intell. **87**(1–2), 343–385 (1996)
12. Scannapieco, M., Catarci, T.: Data quality under a computer science perspective. Arch. Comput. **2**, 1–15 (2002)
13. Wand, Y., Wang, R.Y.: Anchoring data quality dimensions in ontological foundations. Commun. ACM **39**(11), 86–95 (1996)
14. Wijsen, J.: Temporal integrity constraints. In: Liu, L., Özsu, M.T. (eds.) Encyclopedia of Database Systems, pp. 2976–2982. Springer, Boston (2009). https://doi.org/10.1007/978-0-387-39940-9
15. Yu, Y., Zhu, Y., Li, S., Wan, D.: Time series outlier detection based on sliding window prediction. Math. Probl. Eng. **1**, 1–14 (2014)

# Data-Intensive Computing Acceleration with Python in Xilinx FPGA

Yalin Yang, Linjie Xu, Zichen Xu, and Yuhao Wang[⊠]

School of Information Engineering, Nanchang University, Nanchang, China
{yalinyang,linjiexu}@email.ncu.edu.cn, {xuz,wangyuhao}@ncu.edu.cn

**Abstract.** Data-intensive workloads drive the development of hardware design. Such data intensive services are driven the raising trend of novel machine learning techniques, such as CNN/RNN, over massive chunks of data objects. These services require novel devices with configurable high throughput in I/O (i.e., data-based model training), and uniquely large computation capability (i.e., large number of convolutional operations). In this paper, we present our early work on realizing a python-based Field-Programmable Gate Array (FPGA) system to support such data-intensive services. In our current system, we deploy a light layer of CNN optimization and a mixed hardware setup, including multiple FPGA/GPU nodes, to provide performance acceleration on the run. Our prototype can support popular machine learning platform, such as Caffe, etc. Our initial empirical results show that our system can perfect handling all data-intensive learning services.

**Keywords:** Data intensive · FPGA · Python · PYNQ

## 1 Introduction

Artificial Intelligence (AI) has become a hot research topic in recent years, and not only that, neural networks, machine learning, deep learning and heterogeneous computing are also frequently seen in these years' works [20, 21]. With the introduction of deep learning and the improvement of algorithm networks, artificial intelligence is applied in all aspects of life. As models in machine learning become more and more complex, there exist a huge demand for faster hardware and on which, easier deployment.

One good example is, using general purpose graphic processing unit (GPGPU) as a co-processor [32–35], in order to speed up such process. The starting point of GPGPU design is to adapt to high-intensity, multi-parallel computing. It is mainly good at parallel computing like image processing, which is called "coarse-grain parallelism". GPGPU provides a large number of computing units and a large amount of high-speed memory, allowing multiple pixels to be processed in parallel at the same time. However, the structure of the GPGPU chip determines that it is the same as the instruction execution process of the CPU. It fetches instructions, decodes instructions, and executes instructions.

© Springer Nature Switzerland AG 2019
H. Hacid et al. (Eds.): QUAT 2018, LNCS 11235, pp. 111–124, 2019.
https://doi.org/10.1007/978-3-030-19143-6_8

The computational unit only works when the instructions are executed. Therefore, GPGPU does not fully utilize floating-point computing power. In addition, introducing the GPGPU with thousands of cores inevitably raises the demand for power supply, cooling, and capital costs.

To address these challenges, Field-Programmable Gate Array (FPGA) is gradually entering the field of computational acceleration due to its low cost and low power consumption [36,41–44]. The FPGA contains internal input and output blocks (IOBs), configurable logic blocks (CLBs), static random access memories (SRAMs), and digital clock managers (DCMs). Unlike CPU and GPU architectures, FPGAs implement user-defined algorithms directly through transistor circuits without translation through the instruction system. Therefore, when processing large amounts of data, FPGA has excellent parallel processing performance and comparable computing performance to GPGPU [27–31]. But the FPGA is not perfect, compared to GPGPU, popular machine learning frameworks, such as Tensorflow [17], Caffe [18], PyTorch [19], etc., are hard to be deployment onto such hardware. The foremost challenge of using FPGA for data-intensive modeling process is fast and easy model deployment. In addition, because FPGAs are algorithmically programmed in hardware language, this requires designers to have knowledge of FPGA hardware implementations, which increases the barrier to entry for FPGAs. It creates a barrier for potential software designers to try to use FPGA accelerators and other applications. And this barrier has limited the development of the FPGA developer community and has led to slow development of FPGA applications.

In recent years, Python has become one of the most popular programming languages [1]. From Fig. 1 we can see that the usage rate of Python has continued to increase since 2004, and the growth rate has intensified. Python can be the glue that binds together software and hardware developers, not only because it has a rich and powerful library to be used, but more importantly, Python is widely used in data-intensive machine learning, with unparalleled expandability and portability.

We examine a released Python tool, called PYNQ (PYthon on zyNQ) [2], as our environment in order to verify the acceleration of data-intensive services in FPGA. The platform benefits from Python, including tools and libraries with the function of programmable logic and ARM processors. But the PYNQ officially supported devices only pynq-z1, z2 and recently added ZCU104 [2]. We ported the PYNQ platform to the Xilinx ZYNQ-7000 ZC706, which includes the Xilinx XC7Z045 FFG900-2 SOC, with 1 GB of DDR3 memery and 2X16MB Quad SPI Flash. The Zynq- 7000 also integrated ARM dual-core Cortex-A9 processor which could achieve a faster data calculation and processing than most other official pynq devices. Our initial empirical results show that our system can perfect handling all data-intensive learning services.

In next section, we briefly describe related work, based on which we build up our study. In Sect. 3, the design of our work is clearly explained. Section 4, before we come to our conclusion, presents our experimental process and results.

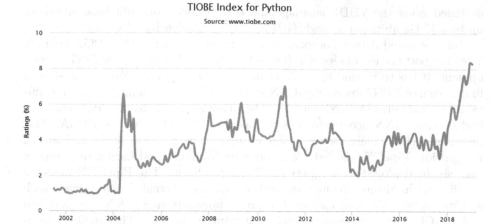

**Fig. 1.** Python language usage since 2002

## 2  Related Work

Data-intensive services, such as machine learning and model training, are the driving force for todays domain-specific architecture. With a better hardware architecture, the performance and quality of the data service can be estimated. Our work adds to the field of examining the performance of data services in modern co-processors, such as FPGA.

After the first FPGA chip was introduced in 1985, FPGAs have been moving forward at a fast and steady pace. In recent years, FPGAs have always led the way. The market prospects for FPGAs are extremely attractive, but the high threshold for Research and development is unmatched in the chip industry. Xilinx and Altera share nearly ninety percent of the market, with more than 6,000 patents. Research on the application development of FPGAs in deep learning has never stopped.

The traditional FPGA development environment [22–24] includes VHDL (Very High Speed Integrated Circuit Hardware Description Language), Verilog HDL (Hardware Description Language) and C/C++, because of there are no neural network related library functions for developers to call, developers have to write their own, which is obviously not friendly to the development of neural morphology calculation and these functions written by different developers are also not flexible to use, lacking good universality and portability. Therefore, it's necessary to explore a new system to support these data intensive services.

The 8-bit fixed-point parallel multiply-accumulate (MAC) cell architecture proposed by Hossam O. Ahmed of Ain-Shams University in Cairo, Egypt, aims to create a fully customized MAC unit for Convolutional Neural Networks (CNN) instead of relying on traditional digital signal processing (DSP) modules and embedded memory cells for FPGA fabric silicon fabrics [26]. The proposed 8-bit fixed-point parallel multiply-accumulate (MAC) cell architecture is designed using the VHDL language and can perform computational speeds of up to 4.17 Gigabits per second (GOPS) using high-density FPGAs.

Intel acquired Altera Corporation as a major supplier in the FPGA field [9]. They support the use of OpenCL (Open Computing Language) for FPGA development. It has to be said that this is an excellent response. Wang et al. show a first design of FPGA-based PipeCNN model [10], which is a large-scale convolutional neural network (CNN) model. The primary goal is to provide a common and efficient CNN accelerator design based on OpenCL on the FPGA. This design model is widely used in image classification, video analysis, and speech recognition. PipeCNN is scalable in both performance and hardware resources and can be deployed on a variety of FPGA platforms. The PipeCNN model is an efficient hardware architecture with a pipelined kernel. These kernels such as Convolution, Pooling, and local response normalization (LRN) are designed in OpenCL's heterogeneous parallel computing framework. This architecture is implemented in the FPGA to effectively reduce memory footprint and bandwidth requirements to improve performance.

The solution given by Xilinx, another major supplier of FPGA, is PYNQ which is a development environment. In recent work [3–8], they show that using Python exhibits reasonably good performance in FPGA. Schmidt [8] used the Python development environment to evaluate the devices impact, performance results, and bottlenecks of FPGA when programming applications for Xilinx Zynq devices using the Python language. The results show that the PYNQ implementation is 30 times faster than the C language, and even more when Python implementations use more efficient available libraries, such as OpenCV, the performance can grow even more.

Inspired by these articles [3–8], we chose Python as our development language. However unlike previous works, which allow application developers to describe hardware kernels (and even entire systems) using low-level python code, we chose the PYNQ platform, that these hardware kernels have been incorporated into PYNQ overlays, to complete our research. The feature of PYNQ greatly shorten the development cycle and lower the threshold for development.

## 3   Design

There are many custom development languages for FPGA, including VHDL and Verilog HDL, as well as C/C++, but they are not ideal for performing data-intensive tasks [8]. Python as a programming language has been highly praised by algorithmic engineers around the world, and more and more people are coming into contact with and using Python. Therefore, the introduction of the Xilinx PYNQ platform inspired us to use Python language as the development language of FPGA to carry out our work.

PYNQ is an open source project for Xilinx that allows people to quickly design embedded systems using Python languages and libraries. Particularly using Python, developers can use hardware libraries and overlays on the programmable logic. Hardware libraries, or overlays, can speed up software running on a Zynq board, and customize the hardware platform and interfaces. PYNQ is more convenient to use than traditional FPGA development tools and platforms. It includes interactive debuggers qdb, as well as many common Python libraries and packages, such as NumPy, SciPy, and matplotlib. Otherwise, the PYNQ image currently includes drivers for the most commonly used USB webcams, WiFi peripherals, and other standard USB devices, these make real-time data acquisition and processing more convenient and simple, as shown in Fig. 2.

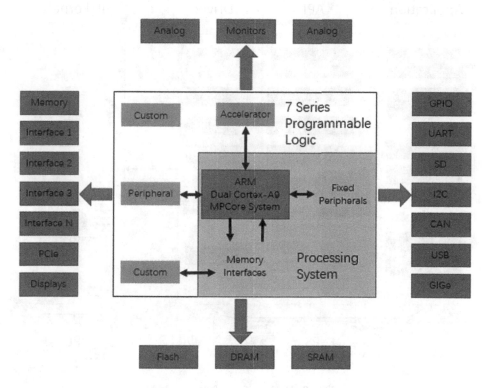

**Fig. 2.** Design of our framework

Through overlays or hardware libraries, we can extend applications from Zynq's processing system to programmable logic. Overlays can be used to speed up software applications or to customize hardware platforms for specific applications. PYNQ provides a Python interface that allows Python to run from the PS to control the overlay in the PL. The PYNQ overlay is created by the hardware designer and included in this PYNQ Python API. Software developers can then use the Python interface to program and control dedicated hardware coverage without having to design their own coverage.

The hardware device we use is the board of the Xilinx Zynq-7000 series which is not officially supported by the PYNQ project. But in theory, it is possible to use PYNQ with any other Zynq development boards. We need to download the source files to rebuild the PYNQ image for our boards from PYNQ GitHub. Then write the compiled PYNQ image to the microSD card minimum 8 GB recommended. PYNQ runs on Linux which uses the following Zynq PS peripherals by the microSD card to boot the system and host the Linux file system, and connects to the Jupyter notebook via Ethernet and accesses the Linux terminal via the UART. Details of our design can be seen on Fig. 2.

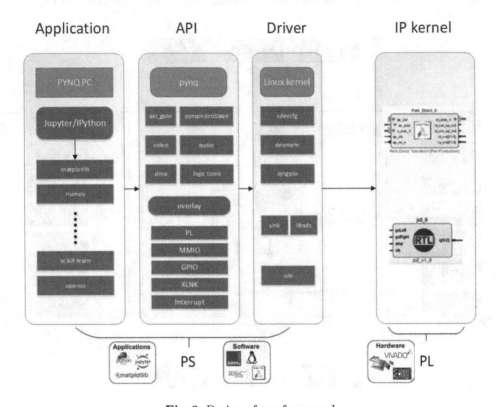

**Fig. 3.** Design of our framework

The design of the whole system is mainly divided into two parts: processing system (PS) and programmable logic (PL). The PS part mainly completes the scheduling and preprocessing of the data, and realizes the control of the PL data stream which downloads the input feature map (IFM) to the PL for calculation acceleration by calling the driver of PYNQ, and the output feature map (OFM) of the accelerated calculation is also returned to the PS through DDR, as shown in Fig. 3.

The Jupyter notebook is a browser based interactive computing environment that enables developers to creat their works include live code, plots, images and video. The Zynq board that supports PYNQ can be easily programmed on the Jupyter notebook using Python.

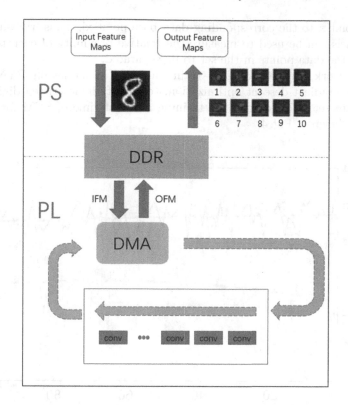

**Fig. 4.** PS, PL data flow diagram of our framework

## 4   Experiments

As python is popular in real application environment of AI, our experiments are carried out with the python-based framework. PYNQ [2] is an official package that enables python programming on FPGA. Previous work [8,37–40] has showed the stability and capability of PYNQ on FPGA. Moreover, There were some data-intensive works based on PYNQ released recently. Such as Machine Learning on distributed clusters [14]and some deep learning framework [15]. In order to evaluate the performance of using Python and PYNQ for data intensive task, we have chosen three common typical data intensive task, SVM [16], Full Connection Network [13], Convolutional-based neural network [12].

### 4.1   Classification on SVM

We first examine the classic machine learning model-support vector machine [16] (SVM). To test SVM on our heterogeneous platform which combined by FPGA and ARM processor, we set a target by the following equation $\sum_i a_i k(x_i, x) = constant$ here $k(x_i, x)$ is a function negatively correlated to the distance between $x_i$ and $x$. As it becomes smaller, then each of the sums is a measure of how close the test point x to the corresponding data base point xi. Thus, the sum of the above kernels can be used to measure the relative proximity of each test point relative to the data points in the set to be separated.

In this work, we are going to train an L2-SVM model on PYNQ using stochasting gradient descent optimization, to classify handwritten digits of the MNIST data set. We recorded the training and test time of SVM for the first five epoch shown in Fig. 4.

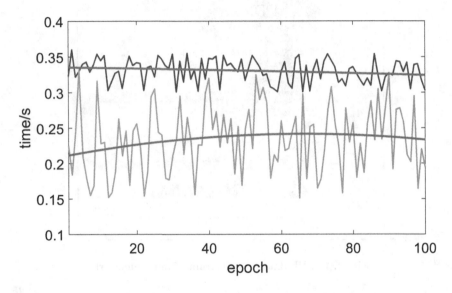

**Fig. 5.** Blue, green fold line show the train time and test time of our SVM model. And red curve shows the trends of time consumption. (Color figure online)

We are going to perform training on both the CPU and the FPGA, comparing performance. As shown in Table 1.

**Table 1.** The comparing of CPU and FPGA.

| Devices | Training time(s/epoch) | Test time(s) | Accuracy |
|---------|------------------------|--------------|----------|
| CPU     | 21.87                  | 0.46         | 0.9002   |
| FPGA    | 0.52                   | 0.13         | 0.9004   |

## 4.2    Simple Classification on Deep Learning

To test the ability to process large scale of data, we design a full connection network on two classes classification. For rendering datasets, we randomized 100 million 2-dimension vectors in two classes. These vectors we write as $x_i$ and

$y_i$ as their class. In this condition our task can be written as $F(X) \rightarrow Y$ in which $F(x) = f_1(f_2(..f_k(x)..))$ and $f_i(x) = Wx + b$. $W$ here is a parameter matrix represents a single network layer. The loss function is cross-entropy [25] (Table 2):

$$loss() = ylog(\hat{y}) + (1 - y)log(1 - \hat{y})$$

**Table 2.** Configuration of full connection network.

| #Layers | #Units | bias | #Layers | #Units | bias |
|---------|--------|------|---------|--------|------|
| 1 | 125 | Yes | 5 | 500 | Yes |
| 2 | 125 | Yes | 6 | 256 | Yes |
| 3 | 256 | Yes | 7 | 64 | Yes |
| 4 | 256 | Yes | 8 | 1 | No |

The average time spent on training and testing the 4 and 8 layers of a full connection network for 100 epochs was calculated and shown in Table 3.

**Table 3.** The training and test time of full connection network.

| Layers | Training time(s/epoch) | Test time(s) |
|--------|------------------------|--------------|
| 4 | 12.32 | 0.53 |
| 8 | 40.83 | 1.12 |

### 4.3 Image Classification on CNN

Convolution-based neural network (CNN) requires great computation power for the large scale of input data, images or videos.

Here we trained a CNN model on MNIST dataset [11], which includes 60,000 train images and 10,000 test images. The task can be defined as $f(x) \rightarrow y$ in which the $f(x)$ is our CNN model and x is the input, an image. Our purpose is to classify which class the image belongs to, that is, to predict a class y.

A single convolution with one filter can be defined as $f \star g(image) = \sum a_i \star b_i$. Commonly an image has 3 channels (e.g. green, blue, red for a color-channeled image) and if it is in 480p resolution, a single image takes one millions (1,036,800) of bytes to store its pixels. Besides of the massive memory requirements, to take convolution on such a great amount of pixels with many filters costs a great deal of computation power. To simplify our test, we did not use batch normalization that costs more computation power (requires the expectation and variance of output of every layer in a network). The configuration of our CNNs as shown in Fig. 5, and our 6-layer CNNs is on Table 4.

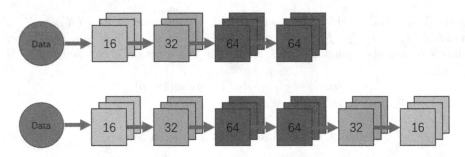

**Fig. 6.** The configuration of our CNNs

**Table 4.** Configuration of CNNs.

| Layers | Units | Kernel size | Stride | Layers | Units | Kernel size | Stride |
|--------|-------|-------------|--------|--------|-------|-------------|--------|
| 1 | 16 | 3 | 1 | 4 | 64 | 3 | 1 |
| 2 | 32 | 3 | 1 | 5 | 32 | 3 | 1 |
| 3 | 64 | 3 | 1 | 6 | 16 | 3 | 1 |

We recorded the time consumption of training and testing the 4 and 6 layers of Convolutional-based neural network for 100 epochs, and calculated the average time, as shown in Table 5.

**Table 5.** The training and test time of CNNs.

| Layers | Training time(s/epoch) | Test time(s) |
|--------|------------------------|--------------|
| 4 | 25.5 | 2.01 |
| 6 | 48.0 | 3.28 |

### 4.4    Image Classification on LeNet-5

LeNet-5 is a convolutional neural network designed by Yann LeCun for handwritten digit recognition in 1998 [30] and is one of the most representative experimental systems in early convolutional neural networks. LeNet-5 has 7 layers (excluding the input layer), each layer containing a different number of training parameters. The structure of each layer is shown in Fig. 6.

The main types of LeNet-5 are convolutional layer, pooled layer and fully connected layer. The convolutional layer uses a 5 × 5 convolution kernel, and the convolution kernel has a sliding step size of one pixel at a time. The pooling layer uses a 2 × 2 input field, and the upper 4 nodes serve as input to the next layer of 1 node, and the input fields do not overlap, that is, 2 pixels per slide (Fig. 7).

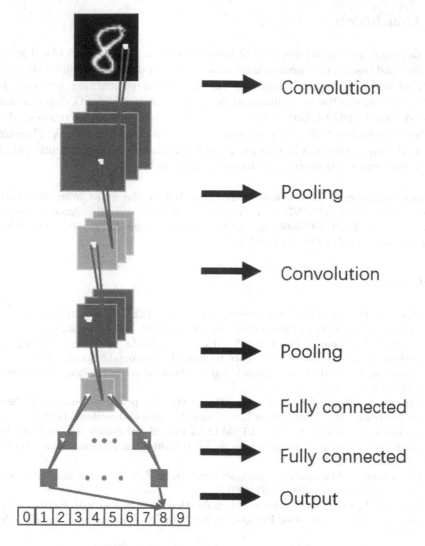

**Fig. 7.** The configuration of LeNet-5

We recorded the time consumption of training and testing the LeNet-5 on MNIST dataset [11] for 100 epochs, and calculated the average time, as shown in Table 6.

**Table 6.** The training and test time of LeNet-5.

| Devices | Training time(s/epoch) | Test time(s) |
|---------|------------------------|--------------|
| CPU     | 218.3                  | 13.1         |
| FPGA    | 17.2                   | 0.9          |

## 5 Conclusion

In this paper, we applied our PYNQ-based prototype on novel FPGAs. Through training and testing of representative models, we validate the stability and capability of our prototype on handling all data-intensive learning services. The prototype contributes as a universal develop tools and benefits data-intensive tasks on novel FPGAs. But there is currently no detailed and accurate study of Python's operational efficiency and energy distribution on the FPGA. Therefore, our next step of research in this direction is to measure, compare and optimize the performance and energy loss based on this prototype.

**Acknowledgement.** This research was supported by the grant from the Tencent Rhino Grant award (11002675), by the grant from the National Science Foundation China (NSFC) (617022501006873), and by the grant from Jiangxi Province Science Foundation for Youths (708237400050).

## References

1. Class, S.: The 2016 Top Programming Languages. IEEE Spectrum (2016)
2. Xilinx: PYNQ: Python Productivity for Zynq (2016). http://www.pynq.io
3. Haglund, P., Mencer, O., Luk, W., Tai, B.: PyHDL: hardware scripting with python. In: International Conference on Field Programmable Logic (2003)
4. Decaluwe, J.: MyHDL: a python-based hardware description language. Linux J. **127**, 84–87 (2004)
5. Logaras, E., Manolakos, E.: SysPy: using python for processorcentric SoC design. In: International Conference on Electronics, Circuits and Systems (2010)
6. Lockhart, D., Zibrat, G., et al.: PyMTL: a unified framework for vertically integrated computer architecture research. In: International Symposium on Microarchitecture (2014)
7. Koromilas, E., Stamelos, I.: Spark acceleration on FPGAs: a use case on machine learning in Pynq. In: MOCAST (2017)
8. Schmidt, A., et al.: Evaluating rapid application development with Python for heterogeneous processor-based FPGAs. In: IEEE International Symposium on FCCM (2017)
9. Intel completes acquisition of altera. https://newsroom.intel.com/news-releases/intel-completes-acquisition-of-altera
10. Wang, D., An, J., Xu, K.: PipeCNN: An OpenCL-Based FPGA Accelerator for Large-Scale Convolution Neuron Networks
11. Xiao, H., Rasul, K., Vollgraf, R.: Fashion-MNIST: a Novel Image Dataset for Benchmarking Machine Learning Algorithms, arXiv:1708.07747 [cs, stat], August 2017
12. Krizhevsky, A., Hinton, G., et al.: ImageNet classification with deep convolutional neural networks. In: Advances in Neural Information Processing Systems (2012)
13. Garson, J. et al.: Connectionism. In: Stanford Encyclopedia of Philosophy
14. Kachris, C., et al.: SPynq: acceleration of machine learning applications over Spark on Pynq. In: 2017 International Conference on (SAMOS). IEEE (2017)
15. Wang, E., Davis, J.J., Cheung, P.: A PYNQ-based Framework for Rapid CNN Prototyping

16. Hearst, M.A., et al.: Support vector machines. IEEE Intell. Syst. Appl. **13**(4), 18–28 (1998)
17. Abadi, M., et al.: Tensorflow: a system for large-scale machine learning. In: OSDI, vol. 16 (2016)
18. Jia, Y., et al.: Caffe: convolutional architecture for fast feature embedding. In: International Conference on Multimedia. ACM (2014)
19. Paszke, A., et al.: Automatic Differentiation in Pytorch (2017)
20. Hinton, G., et al.: Deep neural networks for acoustic modeling in speech recognition: the shared views of four research groups. IEEE Sig. Process. Mag. **29**(6), 82–97 (2012)
21. Topcuoglu, H., Hariri, S., Wu, M.-Y.: Performance-effective and low-complexity task scheduling for heterogeneous computing. IEEE Trans. Parallel Distrib. Syst. **13**(3), 260–274 (2002)
22. Hai, J.C.T., Pun, O.C., Haw, T.W.: Accelerating video and image processing design for FPGA using HDL coder and simulink. In: 2015 IEEE Conference on Sustainable Utilization and Development in Engineering and Technology (CSUDET), pp. 1–5 (2015)
23. Gannot, G., Ligthart, M.: Verilog HDL based FPGA design. In: International Verilog HDL Conference, pp. 86–92 (1994)
24. Rasul, R., et al.: FPGA accelerated computing platform for MATLAB and C/C++. In: 2013 11th International Conference on Frontiers of Information Technology, pp. 166–171 (2013)
25. de Boer, P.-T., et al.: A tutorial on the cross-entropy method. Ann. Oper. Res. **134**, 19–67 (2005)
26. Ahmed, H.O., Ghoneima, M., Dessouky, M.: Concurrent MAC unit design using VHDL for deep learning networks on FPGA. In: 2018 IEEE Symposium on Computer Applications Industrial Electronics (ISCAIE), pp. 31–36 (2018)
27. Nallatech.: FPGA Acceleration of Convolutional Neural Networks (2016)
28. Qiao, Y., Shen, J., Xiao, T., Yang, Q., Wen, M., Zhang, C.: FPGA-accelerated deep convolutional neural networks for high throughput and energy efficiency. Pract. Exp. Concurr. Comput. (2016)
29. Stylianos I Venieris and Christos-Savvas Bouganis.: fpgaConvNet: a framework for mapping convolutional neural networks on FPGAs. In: 2016 IEEE 24th Annual International Symposium on Field-Programmable Custom Computing Machines (FCCM), pp. 40–47. IEEE (2016)
30. Umuroglu, Y., et al.: Finn: a framework for fast, scalable binarized neural network inference. In: Proceedings of the 2017 ACM/SIGDA International Symposium on Field-Programmable Gate Arrays, FPGA 17, pp. 65–74. ACM (2017)
31. Qiu, J., et al.: Going deeper with embedded fpga platform for convolutional neural network. In: Proceedings of the 2016 ACM/SIGDA International Symposium on Field-Programmable Gate Arrays, pp. 26–35. ACM (2016)
32. Che, S., Li, J., Sheaffer, J.W., Skadron, K., Lach, J.: Accelerating compute-intensive applications with GPUs and FPGAs. In: 2008 Symposium on Application Specific Processors, pp. 101–107 (2008)
33. Fan, Z., Qiu, F., Kaufman, A., et al.: GPU cluster for high performance computing. In: Proceedings of the 2004 ACM/IEEE Conference on Supercomputing, p. 47. IEEE Computer Society (2004)
34. Kirk, D.: NVIDIA CUDA software and GPU parallel computing architecture. In: ISMM, vol. 7, pp. 103–104, October 2007
35. Owens, J.D., Houston, M., Luebke, D., Green, S., Stone, J.E., Phillips, J.C.: GPU computing. Proc. IEEE **96**(5), 879–899 (2008)

36. Herbordt, M.C., et al.: Achieving high performance with FPGA-based computing. Computer **40**(3), 50–57 (2007)
37. Kachris, C., Koromilas, E., Stamelos, I., Soudris, D.: FPGA acceleration of spark applications in a Pynq cluster. In: 2017 27th International Conference on Field Programmable Logic and Applications (FPL), p. 1. IEEE, September 2017
38. Koromilas, E., Stamelos, I., Kachris, C., Soudris, D.: Spark acceleration on FPGAs: a use case on machine learning in Pynq. In: 2017 6th International Conference on Modern Circuits and Systems Technologies (MOCAST), pp. 1–4. IEEE, May 2017
39. Janßen, B., Zimprich, P., Hübner, M.: A dynamic partial reconfigurable overlay concept for PYNQ. In: 2017 27th International Conference on Field Programmable Logic and Applications (FPL), pp. 1–4. IEEE, September 2017
40. Stornaiuolo, L., Santambrogio, M., Sciuto, D.: On how to efficiently implement deep Learning algorithms on PYNQ platform. In: 2018 IEEE Computer Society Annual Symposium on VLSI (ISVLSI), pp. 587–590. IEEE, July 2018
41. Gokhale, M., Stone, J., Arnold, J., Kalinowski, M.: Stream-oriented FPGA computing in the streams-C high level language. In: 2000 IEEE Symposium on Field-Programmable Custom Computing Machines, pp. 49–56. IEEE (2000)
42. Gokhale, M., Minnich, R.: FPGA computing in a data parallel C. In: IEEE Workshop on FPGAs for Custom Computing Machines, 1993, Proceedings, pp. 94–101. IEEE, April 1993
43. Hauck, S., DeHon, A.: Reconfigurable Computing: The Theory and Practice of FPGA-Based Computation, vol. 1. Elsevier (2010)
44. Shirazi, N., Walters, A., Athanas, P.: Quantitative analysis of floating point arithmetic on FPGA based custom computing machines. In: FCCM, p. 0155. IEEE, April 1995

# Delone and McLean IS Success Model
# for Evaluating Knowledge Sharing

Azadeh Sarkheyli[✉] and William Wei Song

Dalarna University, Borlänge, Sweden
{asy, wso}@du.se

**Abstract.** It is generally agreed upon that Knowledge Sharing (KS) is an effective process within organizational settings. It is also the corner-stone of many firm's Knowledge Management (KM) Strategy. Despite the growing significance of KS for organization's competitiveness and performance, analyzing the level of KS make it difficult for KM to achieve the optimum level of KS. Because of these causes, this study attempts to develop a conceptual model based on one of the IS Theories that is determined as the best model for evaluating the level of KS. In other words, it is Delone and McLean IS Success model that is presented according to the Communication Theory and it covers various perspectives of assessing Information Systems (IS). Hence, these dimensions cause it to be a multidimensional measuring model that could be a suitable model for realizing the level of KS.

**Keywords:** Knowledge Sharing · Knowledge Management ·
Knowledge Sharing Quality · Delone and McLean IS Success Model

## 1 Introduction

Definition of Knowledge could be a composition of various tangible and intangible things such as experience, values, expert knowledge, contextual information which are useful for incorporating the new experience and information. Knowledge is more intangible because it exists in person minds and it is demonstrated through their behaviors and actions not only in documents and repositories [1–3].

In the new economy, Knowledge Sharing (KS) as one of the main concepts of Knowledge Management (KM) is very significant for all of the organizations. It is a key process in creating new products and services, in leveraging organizational knowledge assets and in achieving collective outcomes. However, research on KS also revealed its complex nature and a multitude of factors that impede KS in and between organizations.

Although many models are defined for it, many of which are not optimum and initiatives fail. Moreover, the research to date has tended to focus on KS rather than KS assessment. Hence, evaluating the level of KS could very beneficial for IT Managers in order to better decision making for evaluation their existing KS.

Furthermore, data, information and knowledge within the firm as well as using it to increment a competitive advantage in an organization has developed into the field of KM. Accordingly, KM is the collection of processes and tools that comprehensively

© Springer Nature Switzerland AG 2019
H. Hacid et al. (Eds.): QUAT 2018, LNCS 11235, pp. 125–136, 2019.
https://doi.org/10.1007/978-3-030-19143-6_9

capture, organizes, shares, and analyzes knowledge assets which are recognized from resources, documents, and people skills within the organization.

KM initiative is expanding across all types of organizations worldwide and in most of the firms, this started out with a mere investment in communication infrastructure. However, more enterprises are now starting to realize that requires thorough planning and must involve end users. Firms that expand and leverage resources of knowledge achieve more success than firms who are more dependent on tangible resources.

Therefore, the growing use of knowledge in businesses contributed to the emergence of the theory of KM, which is currently one of the hottest topics in IT and management literature [4]. In this research, we will use two phases of research approach.

Thus, the first phase that is presented in this paper, aims to develop general research model and a conceptual framework. The second phase entails the development of a survey, based on phase one, and the use of the questionnaire in an empirical study.

In the next section, we discuss the KS understanding and its model and success criteria. In Sect. 3, Delone and McLean Model is presented as a means of IS Success Factors. This is followed by a presentation of the proposed conceptual framework in order to provide a support of evaluation of the KS Level. In the final section, we present conclusion and future research.

## 2   Understanding Knowledge Sharing

The process of KM involves several activities. However, the most commonly discussed activity in the process of KM nowadays is knowledge transfer (knowledge sharing) [5]. Knowledge transfer in an organization occurs when members of an organization pass knowledge to each other.

Hence, Nonaka and Takeuchi propose four modes of knowledge creation and transfer that are specified as Socialization, Externalization, Combination, and Internalization (see Fig. 1 and Table 1) [6].

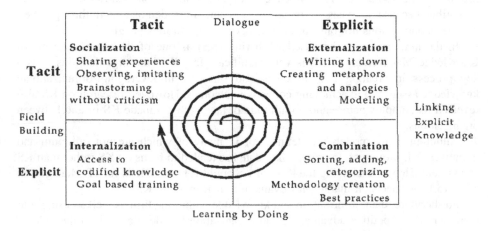

**Fig. 1.** Procedures of KS [6]

**Table 1.** Four modes of knowledge creation and transfer [6]

| Modes | Describe |
|---|---|
| Socialization | It is the process of sharing experiences and thereby creating tacit knowledge such as mental models and technical skills. Tacit knowledge can be obtained without using the language through observation, imitation, and practice |
| Externalization | It is the process of articulating tacit knowledge in the form of explicit concepts, taking the shapes of metaphors, analogies, concepts, hypotheses, or models |
| Combination | It is the process of systemizing concepts into a knowledge system by combining different bodies of explicit knowledge. Explicit knowledge is transferred through media such as documents, meetings, email, and/or phone conversations. Categorization of this knowledge can lead to the generation of new knowledge |
| Internalization | It is the process of converting explicit knowledge to tacit knowledge and is closely related to learning by doing |

## 2.1 Knowledge Sharing Models

In general, models represent a reality and most of the KS models are theoretical which present the related process or mechanism that has been developed to describe a phenomenon. There are several KS models that are suggested by researchers. The varieties of existing models due to diverse researchers focus KS from different perspectives. Some of the KS models/frameworks address the qualifications or factors influencing KS whilst the others address the relationship between KS and performance [7].

Hence, literature in KS shows that KS models are diverse. In other words, a variety of models exist as the results of differing views on a subject which is broad and subjective. Thus, most of the researchers addressed critical factors of KS rather than the relationship between KS and performance.

Therefore, this study by focusing on both views of models could be very useful for improving the KS quality. Accordingly, the general dimensions of all KS models are identified as Individual, Organizational, Technological, KS quality, Organizational Performance, and Service Delivery [7].

On the other hand, although all of the identified dimensions of KS could be significant, there is little discussion about KS quality that has been addressed by researchers of KM/KS (see Fig. 2) [7].

## 2.2 Knowledge Sharing Critical Success Factors

Many authors have attempted to draw up a comprehensive list of critical success factors (CSFs) for successful implementation of KS in different study contexts. Some of them are mentioned in this study. However, Table 2 is created to show the comparison of KS CSFs studying in the literature.

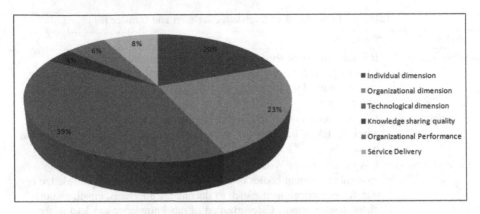

**Fig. 2.** Comparison of the KS dimensions

**Table 2.** Comparison of KS CSFs proposing in other studies

| Author | KS CSFs |
|---|---|
| Gupta and Govindarajan [8] | • Information systems (IS)<br>• People<br>• Process<br>• Leadership<br>• Reward system<br>• Organizational structure |
| Hung *et al.* [9] | • Leadership of senior management<br>• Information technology<br>• Reward and motivation<br>• Organizational culture and structure<br>• Training |
| Alavi *et al.* [10, 11] | • Trust<br>• Communication between staff<br>• IS<br>• Reward system<br>• Organizational structure |
| Bishop *et al.* [12] | • Leadership<br>• Rewards<br>• Information technology<br>• Communication<br>• Culture |
| Egbu, et al. [13] | • Management leadership and support<br>• Motivation<br>• Reward and recognition<br>• Trust and relation<br>• Communication and training between staff<br>• Technology and IS<br>• Organizational structure |

Other studies have also reviewed, based on various study contexts, different CSFs that can aid and lead to effective KS among individuals in an organization. While there are some similarities in the studies, they cannot be generalized.

However, by reviewing the CSFs of KS, some of them are selected as the major factors which are listed below (Table 3).

**Table 3.** The selected critical success factors of KS

| CSFs | Description |
| --- | --- |
| Trust and relation | Interpersonal trust or trust between co-workers is an essential attribute in organizational culture, which is believed to have a strong influence on knowledge sharing. Interpersonal trust is known as an individual or a group's expectancy in the reliability of the promise or actions of other individuals or groups [13]. Team members require the existence of trust in order to respond openly and share their knowledge [14] |
| Communication and training between staff | The communication here refers to human interaction through oral conversations and the use of body language while communicating. Human interaction is greatly enhanced by the existence of social networking in the workplace. This form of communication is fundamental in encouraging knowledge transfer [15] |
| Technology and IS | The term information systems are used to refer to an arrangement of people, data and processes that interact to support daily operations, problem-solving and decision making in organizations [16]. Organizations use different IS to facilitate knowledge sharing through creating or acquiring knowledge repositories, where employees share expertise electronically and access to shared experience becomes possible for other staff [17] |
| Reward and motivation | According to Syed-Ikhsan and Rowland [18], employees need a strong motivator in order to share knowledge. It is unrealistic to assume that all employees are willing to easily offer knowledge without considering what may be gained or lost as a result of this action. Managers must consider the importance of collaboration and share best practices when designing reward systems. The idea is to introduce processes in which sharing information and horizontal communication are encouraged and indeed rewarded. Such rewards must be based on a group rather than individual performance [19] |
| Organizational culture and structure | KM fully mediates the impact of organizational culture on organizational effectiveness, and partially mediates the impact of organizational structure and strategy on organizational effectiveness [20] |
| Leadership and senior management | Senior Management support including allocation of resources, leadership, and providing training [21, 22]. Leadership is responsible for practicing strategic planning in making the best use of resources and fostering a knowledge sharing and a learning culture [23] |

## 2.3    Importance of Knowledge Sharing in the Organizations

While traditional KM emphasis was placed on technology or the ability to build systems that efficiently process and leverage knowledge, the new model of KM involves people and actions. It aims at creating an environment where power equals sharing knowledge rather than keeping it. Knowledge transfer requires that an individual or a group cooperate with others to share knowledge and achieve mutual benefits [18].

Consequently, KS is critical to a firm's success as it leads to faster knowledge deployment to portions of the organization that can greatly benefit from it [18, 24]. However, KS assessment should be considered in order to enhance KS and KM in the organization. Hence, in this research, an IS success model is used to evaluate the level of KS.

## 3    Delone and McLean IS Success Model

IS Success is a multidimensional concept for measuring the complex dependent variable in IS research. It is defined as developing the IS success models/frameworks such as D&M which is one of the best models presenting in the paper [25, 26].

Delone and McLean IS Success Model (D&M Model) as an IS Theory is to provide a general and comprehensive definition of IS success that covers different perspectives of evaluating IS, Delone and McLean reviewed the existing definitions of IS success and their corresponding measures and classified them into six major categories. Thus, they created a multidimensional measuring model with interdependencies between the different success categories.

Motivated by Delone and McLean's call for further development and validation of their model, many researchers have attempted to extend or improve the original model. Ten years after the publication of their first model and based on the evaluation of the many contributions to it, Delone and McLean proposed an updated IS success model [25, 26].

The updated model consists of six interrelated dimensions of IS success: information, system and service quality, (intention to) use, user satisfaction, and net benefits (see Table 4).

Table 4. Dependent and independent variables of D&M Model

| Main independent factors | Main dependent factors |
|---|---|
| Knowledge/information quality | Net benefits |
| Service quality | (Intention to) use |
| System quality | User satisfaction |
| | KS quality |

The arrows demonstrate proposed associations between the success dimensions. The model can be interpreted as a system that can be evaluated in terms of information, system, and service quality. Hence, these characteristics affect the subsequent use or intention to use and user satisfaction. As a result of using the system, certain benefits will be achieved.

The net benefits will (positively or negatively) influence user satisfaction and the further use of the IS [25, 26]. Diagram/schematic of the theory shows in Fig. 3 [25].

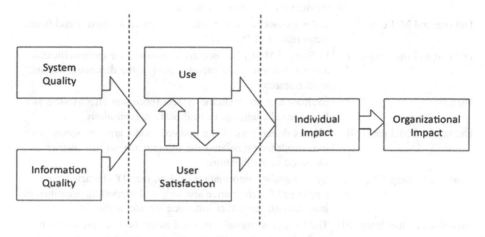

**Fig. 3.** Delone and McLean IS Success Model, 1992 [25]

IS success Model of Delone and Maclean is validated and it is updated after several years. Figure 4 shows this model as below.

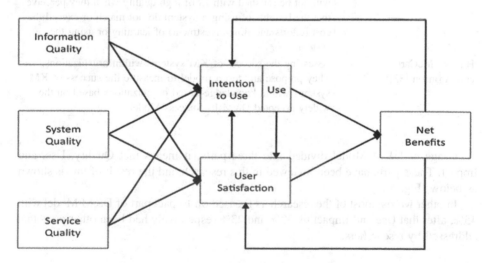

**Fig. 4.** Delone and McLean IS Success Model, 2003 [26]

The model of Delone and McLean has been accepted for several years and has been validated by several studies. The usage of D&M should be reviewed as one of the potential knowledge of the study. Hence a table is created for listing the role of D&M in some of the IS/KM studies. Table 5 shows as below.

**Table 5.** The role of D&M Model in the selected IS/KM studies

| Author | Advantage/usage of D&M |
|---|---|
| DeLone and McLean [25] | Involves of empirical and conceptual measures in order to measure the organization impacts |
| DeLone and McLean [26] | Make a series of recommendations regarding current and future measurement of IS success |
| DeLone and McLean [27] | IS Success Model has become a standard for the specification and justification of the measurement of the dependent variable in IS research |
| Hu [28] | Evaluation of telemedicine system success or effectiveness as a fundamental challenge to healthcare organizations |
| DeLone and McLean [29] | The six dimensions of the updated model are a parsimonious framework for organizing the e-commerce success metrics identified in the literature |
| Bharati and Berg [30] | System quality, information quality, user IT characteristics, employee IT performance and technical support are identified as important elements that influence service quality |
| Bharati and Chaudhury [31] | The IS success model was used as the basis of the research model to impact on different components of user satisfaction such as interface satisfaction, decision-making satisfaction, and resultant overall satisfaction |
| Chae [32] | D&M assumes that the information quality, system quality, and service quality automatically generate user satisfaction. Users will not be satisfied with IS of high quality when they perceive that the benefits of using a system do not match or exceed the cost (efforts and time-investment) of learning or using the system |
| Halawi, McCarthy and Aronson [33] | Assessing the success of KM systems within organizations. They propose and test a model to measure the success of KM systems within knowledge-based organizations based on the widely accepted D&M IS Success Model |

Usage of D&M Model divided into three parts, it means that Quality, Use, and Impact. These parts have been reviewed in this research and the result of this is shown as below (Fig. 5).

In other words, most of the researchers focused on Impact part of D&M Model with 45%, after that Use and Impact by 32% and 23% respectively had been other parts that addressed by researchers.

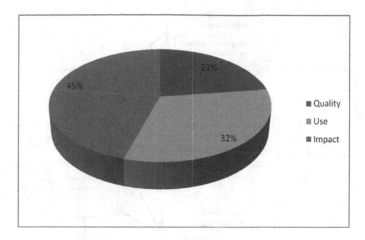

**Fig. 5.** The percentage of usage of D&M Model in three parts

## 4 Developing the Conceptual Framework

The research tends to suggest a component of KS Quality to D&M IS Success Model for evaluating the level of KS. As it has been mentioned before, the advantages of D&M have been used by several researchers.

The usage of D&M is related to the measurement of IS success, it means that, User Satisfaction, Information Quality, Service Quality, System Quality.

Consequently, based on the review of the previous studies in the literature, there are various evaluations through using D&M such as the existing components and other measurements related to the other researchers scopes, for instance, e-commerce success metrics, evaluating telemedicine system success, assessing the success of KM systems, understand factors that impact Decision Making satisfaction in web-based Decision Support systems, User IT Characteristics and identified the IT performance.

Hence, evaluating the level of KS has not been considered in the D&M IS Success Model especially, so in this study assessing the level of KS as one of the dimensions of IS success will be recommended to D&M model.

Thus, a conceptual model is developed for evaluating the level of KS that has been shown in Figs. 6 and 7.

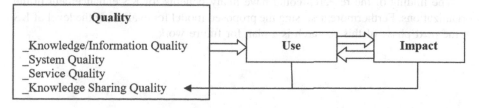

**Fig. 6.** General model for evaluating the level of KS

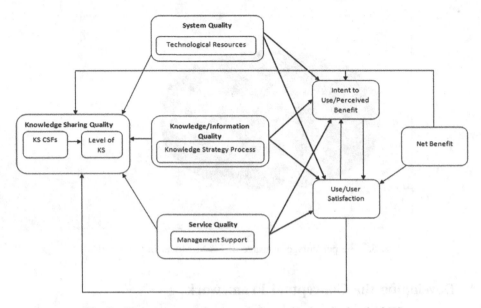

**Fig. 7.** The conceptual framework for evaluating the level of KS

## 5  Conclusion and Future Research

Finding the relationship between the evaluating KS level and IS Success variables which are specified in D&M IS Success model is the main goal of the study. The research was conducted in three different sections. The first part was concerned with discusses generally the role of D&M. During the second phase explains the lack of KS evaluation researches based on the literature. In the third phase, the findings were discussed as a conceptual model which is proposed in the paper. Therefore, KS quality as one of the dependent variables has been added to the D&M IS Success Model.

Finally, based on the conceptual model of IS Success model for KS evaluation, assessing the level of KS, System Quality, Service Quality, Information/Knowledge Quality, Net Benefit and user/user satisfaction will be used. Consequently, KS quality as a dependent variable as like as intent to use/perceived benefit and user/user satisfaction could be measured by all of the dependent and independent variables that are considered.

The finding of the research could have many benefits for KS enhancement in the organizations. Furthermore assessing the proposed model for evaluating the level of KS at the next phase of this research is a plan for future work.

# References

1. Gammelgaard, J., Ritter, T.: Knowledge retrieval process in multinational consulting firms. Danish Social Sciences Research Council, Frederiksberg, Denmark (2000). http://web.cbs. dk/departments/int/seminarpapers/JG-Knowledge.pdf. Accessed 10 Sept 2016
2. Asllani, A., Luthans, F.: What knowledge managers really do: an empirical and comparative analysis. J. Knowl. Manag. **7**(3), 53–66 (2003)
3. Gold, A.H., Malhotra, A., Segars, A.H.: Knowledge management: an organizational capabilities perspective. J. Manag. Inf. Syst. **18**(1), 185–214 (2001)
4. Aranda, D., Fernandez, L.: Determinants of innovation through a knowledge-based theory lens. Ind. Manag. Data Syst. **102**(5), 289–296 (2002)
5. Ford, D.: Trust and knowledge management: the seeds of success. Queen's KBE Center for Knowledge-Based Enterprises, Queen's University, Kingston, ON, Canada (2001). http:// business.queensu.ca/knowledge/workingpapers/working/working_01-08.pdf. Accessed 10 Sept 2016
6. Nonaka, I., Takeuchi, H.: The Knowledge Creating Company: How the Japanese Companies Create the Dynamics of Innovation. Oxford University Press, New York (1995)
7. Sarkheyli, A., Alias, R.A., Ithnin, N., Esfahani, M.D.: Dimensions of knowledge sharing quality: an empirical investigation. J. Res. Innov. Inf. Syst. **3**, 9–18 (2013)
8. Gupta, A.K., Govindarajan, V.: Knowledge management social dimension: lessons from Nucor Steel. Sloan Manag. Rev. **42**(1), 71–81 (2000)
9. Hung, Y.H., Chou, S.C.: On constructing a knowledge management pyramid model. In: IRI-2005 IEEE International Conference on Information Reuse and Integration, Conf, 2005, pp. 1–6. IEEE (2005)
10. Alavi, M., Leidner, D.E.: Knowledge management systems: emerging views and practices from the field. In: Proceedings of the 32nd Hawaii International Conference on System Sciences. IEEE Computer Society (1999)
11. Alavi, M., Leidner, D.E.: Review: Knowledge management and knowledge management systems: conceptual foundations and research issues. MIS Q. **25**(1), 107–136 (2001)
12. Bishop, J.E., O'Reilly, R.L., Maddox, K., Hutchinson, L.J.: Client satisfaction in a feasibility study comparing face-to-face interviews with telepsychiatry. J. Telemed. Telecare **8**(4), 217–221 (2002)
13. Egbu, J.U., Wood, G., Egbu, C.O.: Critical success factors associated with effective knowledge sharing in the provision of floating support services in sheltered housing for the elderly. In: Proceedings of the 26th Annual ARCOM Conference, pp. 849–857 (2010). Association of Researchers in Construction Management
14. Politis, J.: The connection between trust and knowledge management: what are its implications for team performance. J. Knowl. Manag. **7**(5), 55–66 (2003)
15. Gruenfeld, D.H., Mannix, E.A., Williams, K.Y., Neale, M.A.: Group composition and decision making: how member familiarity and information distribution affect process and performance. Organ. Behav. Hum. Decis. Process. **67**(1), 1–15 (1996)
16. Smith, A., Rupp, W.: Communication and loyalty among knowledge workers: a resource of the firm theory view. J. Knowl. Manag. **6**(3), 250–261 (2002)
17. Whitten, J., Bentley, L., Dittman, K.: System Analysis and Design Methods. McGraw-Hill, New York (2001)
18. Syed-Ikhsan, S., Rowland, F.: Knowledge management in public organizations: a study on the relationship between organizational elements and the performance of knowledge transfer. J. Knowl. Manag. **8**(2), 95–111 (2004)

19. Connelly, C., Kelloway, E.: Predictors of employees' perceptions of knowledge sharing cultures. Lead. Organ. Dev. J. **24**(5), 294–301 (2003)
20. Zheng, W., Yang, B., McLean, G.N.: Linking organizational culture, structure, strategy, and organizational effectiveness: mediating role of knowledge management. J. Bus. Res. **63**(7), 763–771 (2010)
21. Goh, S.: Managing effective knowledge transfer: an integrative framework and some practice implications. J. Knowl. Manag. **6**(1), 23–30 (2002)
22. Jennex, M.E.: Knowledge management systems. Int. J. Knowl. Manag. **1**(2), i–iv (2005)
23. Jennex, M.E.: What is knowledge management. Int. J. Knowl. Manag **1**(4), i–iv (2005)
24. Davenport, T.H., Prusak, L.: Working Knowledge: How Organizations Manage What They Know. Harvard Business School Press, Boston (2000)
25. DeLone, W.H., McLean, E.R.: Information systems success: the quest for the dependent variable. Inf. Syst. Res. **3**, 60–95 (1992)
26. DeLone, W.H., McLean, E.R.: The DeLone and McLean model of information systems success: a ten-year update. J. Manag. Inf. Syst. **19**(4), 9–30 (2003)
27. DeLone, W.H., McLean, E.R.: Information systems success revisited. In: Proceedings of the 35th Annual Hawaii International Conference on System Sciences, HICSS, pp. 2966–2976 (2002)
28. Hu, P.J.-H.: Evaluating telemedicine systems success: a revised model. In: Proceedings of the 36th Annual Hawaii International Conference on System Sciences, p. 8 (2003). https://doi.org/10.1109/hicss.2003.1174379
29. DeLone, W.H., McLean, E.R.: Measuring e-commerce success: applying the DeLone & McLean information systems success model. Int. J. Electron. Commer. **9**(1), 31–47 (2004)
30. Bharati, P., Berg, D.: Managing information technology for service quality: a study from the other side. IT People **16**(2), 183–202 (2003)
31. Bharati, P., Chaudhury, A.: Product customization on the web: an empirical study of factors impacting choiceboard user satisfaction. Inf. Resour. Manag. J. **19**(2), 69–81 (2006)
32. Chae, H.-C.: IS success model and perceived IT value. In: AMCIS 2007 Proceedings. Paper 397 (2007)
33. Halawi, L.A., McCarthy, R.V., Aronson, J.E.: An empirical investigation of knowledge-management systems' success. J. Comput. Inf. Syst. **48**(2), 121–135 (2007)

# Author Index

Printed in the United States
By Bookmasters